LUKE'S

Portrait

of Christ

LUKE'S Portrait of Christ

CHARLES M. LAYMON

WOMAN'S DIVISION OF CHRISTIAN SERVICE
BOARD OF MISSIONS, THE METHODIST CHURCH

Woman's Division of Christian Service
Board of Missions of The Methodist Church
New York, N. Y.

Maps Inside Cover   "Palestine" from *A Life of Jesus* by Edgar J. Goodspeed (New York: Harper & Bros., 1950). Used by permission.

Cover Design and Book Format: Claire Valentine

This book is dedicated to
my mother
Sarah Hinkle Laymon
for whom the cause of missions
was a consuming concern

Supplementary Materials

for use with LUKE'S PORTRAIT OF CHRIST

GUIDE to *Luke's Portrait of Christ*,[1] by Daisy Dozier. Woman's Division of Christian Service. (35 cents)

THE CHOICE,[1] a playlet by Jane Stewart. *Luke's Portrait of Christ*, with its emphasis on Christ's reliance on the Scriptures, helps solve the dilemma of a modern Christian. Woman's Division of Christian Service. (25 cents)

THE GOSPEL OF ST. LUKE [1] (K.J.V.), American Bible Society. (5 cents)

THE GOOD NEWS, *The Gospel of St. Luke* [1] (K.J.V.). Illustrated. American Bible Society. (10 cents)

THE 1959 PRAYER CALENDAR.[1] An Itinerary of Prayer. A guide for the spiritual support of all Methodist missionaries, deaconesses, and Christian workers related to the Board of Missions, and for the projects in which they are engaged around the world. Woman's Division of Christian Service. (60 cents; 3 for $1.50)

---

[1] Order the above materials from Literature Headquarters, 7820 Reading Road, Cincinnati 37, Ohio.

Contents

CONTENTS

Foreword

CHRIST IS THE BEGINNING and the end of the Christian Faith. He is the Alpha and Omega. We believe through him, live by his grace, and come before the eternal Presence in his name. For this reason our knowledge of Christ as found through our study of the Scriptures is of surpassing value.

In this book we shall consider the portrait of Christ in the Gospel of Luke, sometimes known as the Third Gospel because of its position in the New Testament. In order of preferment, however, some would name it first. I do not choose to take sides in such a matter since I share the feeling of one of my teachers who said that her favorite book in the Bible was whichever one she happened to be reading.

We are concerned in these pages with portraiture, rather than with a developing story and a sequence of events. And the portrait is lifted out of the Gospel in which it appears in terms of certain major areas of experience in the life of our Lord—commitment, temptation, the reading of the Scriptures, prayer, the Kingdom, social relations, the material world, the cross, and the Resurrection. To this end we shall journey back and forth throughout Luke's Gospel, selecting situations, sayings, and deeds that are pertinent to those areas. Thus the picture which results will be grounded in the life that was lived, in the Word that became flesh and moved among men.

As we consider Luke's portrait of Christ, it may

be that we shall discover not only new insights into the person of our Lord, but also new dimensions in our own lives as well. This was the purpose of the Incarnation. There was no other way to know and be known, to make clear to all the nature of God and man. To this end, in the fullness of time, God sent his own Son to live on the earth. In him is both the pattern and the power of the life that is eternal.

Charles M. Laymon

Luke's Gospel—
an Individual Portrait

THE STORY OF THE NEW TESTAMENT is the story of Christ. It is he who gives meaning and power to the twenty-seven writings that it contains. From first to last his portrait dominates the record. Even when his person is not immediately under consideration, he is the life that throbs within the message that is proclaimed. Thus the entire book bears a dynamic witness to him.

The Witness of the Gospels

It is the Gospels, however, which directly present the ministry and message of Jesus Christ. These unique documents are without parallel in the re-

1

ligious writings of the world. Their fast-moving narratives of the events which marked our Lord's days in the flesh not only record the past, but also make an evangelistic appeal to those who read them. They have remained through the centuries the greatest single invitation to become a follower of Christ.

Strictly speaking, the Gospels do not provide a life of Jesus as we understand biography today. They include only the highlights of his career as the Messiah. Since their writers were deeply concerned to make converts to the Faith, they present their accounts in such a way that the *message* of his ministry, as it was expressed in deed and word, predominates. And this message is found in the portrait they draw.

Portraiture is a fine art in the Gospels. These writings move beyond photographic likeness to include the meaning of Jesus, both for his own time and for eternity. His story is presented as the work of God in the saving of men from their sins, their weakness, and their fear. As he walked among his fellows, he was both Lord and Christ.

Matthew, Mark, and Luke tell essentially the same story concerning Christ.[1] Common to all three is the experience of the life and teachings of Jesus which the early church shared, as well as a single body of tradition (parables, sayings, miracle stories) covering his ministry, death, and resurrection. The fact that Matthew and Luke together use more than

[1] The Gospel of John also has a witness to bear. Here, however, we are dealing only with the Synoptic Gospels (Matthew, Mark, and Luke) because Luke belongs to this group.

ninety per cent of Mark's material in their writings, much of it in the same words, accounts for a great deal of their similarity. All three bear witness to the one basic faith of the Christian community. Here they stand in stanch agreement. Controversy, heresy, and defection from the truth in that distant day had to come face to face with a united front concerning Christ. Against all attacks, the three Gospels held firm in their central position—and have continued to do so to this very day. Would that the churches in this generation were able to speak out as unitedly when they face modern forms of paganism!

In spite of the unity of the Synoptic Gospels in their portrait of Christ and in their interpretation of the Faith, there are individual differences among them which make each a Gospel according to the author who wrote, compiled, and edited it. Matthew, Mark, and Luke each wrote his individual Gospel, even as each of you might write a "gospel according to you," focusing on those aspects of the life of Jesus which most impress you. The mark of the personality of the author is upon each of them. Each had his exclusive contacts which, in some cases, brought him reminiscences of Christ which the others did not possess. For instance, only Luke is familiar with the parable of the Prodigal Son (Luke 15), while Matthew alone knows the parable of the Last Judgment (Matthew 25).[2] Just as our

[2] Matthew's individual or special material may be estimated at a little less than half of his Gospel, while Luke's is probably a little more than half. Mark's is far less, due to the fact that the other two copy so extensively from him. For additional material

3

information is sometimes determined by the section of the country in which we live, so was theirs. Mark is usually associated with Rome, Matthew with Antioch in Syria, and Luke with the Greco-Roman world in such cities as Ephesus or Corinth.

The fact that the Gospel writers wrote at different times (Mark about A.D. 65-70, Matthew A.D. 85-90, Luke A.D. 88-90) may also have made for variety in their reporting and interpretations. Mark probably was at work shortly after the martyrdom of Peter and Paul at the hands of Nero. It was a time of persecution, and a steadying force was needed in the life of the Church. In the almost immediate future lay the destruction of Jerusalem by the Roman armies. This meant that not only the city of David, but also the fountainhead of Christianity, was to be destroyed. The Faith itself seemed to be threatened in this dreadful calamity which loomed menacingly over the horizon. A statement of the foundations of their belief was needed, and Mark prepared his Gospel to provide it.

Matthew also writes from a particular background which made individual treatment of his material imperative. This makes his Gospel peculiarly his own. He wrote during the reign of the Emperor Domitian (A.D. 81-96) who was later to harass the Church as a persecutor. So violent did Domitian become that the author of the Revelation to John pictured him as one of the two beasts who were the agents of

---

on the individual backgrounds of the Gospels, see the author's *Christ in the New Testament* (Nashville: Abingdon Press, 1958), Chapter 8.

Satan on earth (Revelation 13). In the face of impending persecution, the author of Matthew began to think of the end of the age and the final judgment to such an extent that he may almost be said to have majored in the apocalyptic element in the teachings of Jesus.[3] He also wrote at a time when missionary expansion was needed, continuing the first tremendous effort of the apostle Paul. Accordingly, he stressed this aspect of the Faith and included in his Gospel the Great Commission (Matthew 28: 16-20) which called upon the followers of Jesus to take the gospel to the far corners of the earth.

We shall look shortly at Luke's special concerns at the time he wrote the Third Gospel. But before doing this, we should take note that the particular individuality of each of the Synoptic Gospels is due, in part, to the fact that the authors sought to speak to the immediate needs of the day in which they lived. They had "a calling to fulfill" and they fulfilled it, creatively and specifically.

Luke the Author

We do not know a great deal about Luke himself. Next to the composing of Luke-Acts his greatest distinction was that he was a close friend and travelling companion of the apostle Paul. He is mentioned

[3] As used here *apocalyptic* refers to the expected end of the age and the dramatic judgment which was anticipated at the time of the return of Christ. The wicked would be punished and the saints blessed.

5

with affection as being with the great missionary at the time of his imprisonment, presumably at Rome. Colossians 4:14, Philemon 1:24, and II Timothy 4:11 refer to him, so that he came to be a well-known personage. His presence with Paul toward the end, especially at times when he alone was at the side of his friend, marks him as a courageous man. It is altogether likely that he was the only Gentile to write a New Testament document. Paul called him "Luke the beloved physician," and the use of certain medical terms in his writings is sometimes pointed out as a sign of his profession. Scholars are not now so sure that this particular usage was confined to physicians, however, since the same terms have been found elsewhere in the works of non-medical writers.

In the literature of the time, from the second century on, Luke's authorship of the Gospel is unquestioned.[4] Because he was not an apostle, nor at first a famous personage, there would be no particular reason for attaching his name to writings not his own, as was sometimes done. His literary activity, however, has gained for him the reputation of having penned one of the world's most beautiful works. His style is vivid and dramatic, and the deep piety that he possessed is felt in passage after passage of his document. Such an author would write his own gospel with unusual sensitivity to the issues of his day. And he did!

[4] See Eusebius: *Church History* III, 4.6.

6

Luke Writes a Gospel

In order to understand the Gospel of Luke we must first examine its preface (1:1-4). Here Luke is quite personal. He tells us *why* he wrote, *how* he wrote, and *to whom* he wrote. Thus we can enter into the inner mind and spirit of the man at the very outset, even before reading his material. His purpose was avowedly evangelical, since he was interested in confirming the faith of one named Theophilus. This was witness-bearing, no less. The fact that he referred to Theophilus by the title "Most excellent," may imply that the recipient of his treatise was an important governmental official. On the other hand, it would be unrealistic to limit the audience for whom the Gospel was intended to a single individual. The entire Greek-speaking world—particularly the people who were seeking after truth—was in the author's mind as he wrote. It is interesting to note that the name Theophilus is a combination of two Greek words which, in this form, means "friend of God." This fact may suggest that a broad readership was in Luke's mind; here were both facts and inspiration for all who hungered and thirsted for the living God.

Luke also indicates in the preface something of the manner in which he prepared to write. This is important too. Truth must be sifted and recorded with great care; to handle it carelessly is to be guilty of dishonesty. When it is truth about God, a haphazard treatment is nothing short of profanity. This is the case whether we are making a personal testimony to our faith, or composing a more formal statement of belief. In this instance Luke says that he secured his facts from *eye-witnesses*.

But this alone was not sufficient; he traced his data back and checked upon it from the very beginning, and even this thorough scrutiny did not satisfy this writer's code. He arranged the facts in an orderly sequence so that the result would convince his readers of the certainty of the truth he was recording. To be sure, Luke was not a modern historian with all of the scientific tools of historical and documentary analysis that are ours today. Nevertheless, there is an ideal for presenting fact rather than fancy evidenced in these procedures, which would do justice to any modern writer of history.

One further statement in the preface should be examined. Luke makes mention of the fact that many others had written of these matters which had happened among them. Even so, it seemed good to him also to put his pen to the task. Why was this, we may inquire. An answer should be sought in the special or individual material that Luke alone includes,[5] as well as in the particular emphasis he places upon certain attitudes and ideas in the account.

[5] See previous reference, pp. 3-4.

Luke's Special Concerns

The relation of church and state is an ever present issue. It has been so with Christianity almost from the beginning. It is still true today. We meet it often in regard to governmental support for education, particularly in our denominational schools, as well as in matters pertaining to conscientious objection to military service on the part of some of the members of the several church communions. Missionaries abroad must adjust to governmental regulations which establish restrictions, linguistic and otherwise, that affect the carrying on of their work. There is also the question of the state and freedom of speech which is basically a religious concern. Freedom of speech is a cause which needs continually to be espoused by the Church. All of this means that church and state in the daily pursuit of their respective functions are brought into contact with each other. This contact may be mutually creative, or binding and limiting.

In Luke's day church-state relationships were also very definitely affecting the lives of Christians. Judaism was a permitted religion (*religio licita*); it had status in the Roman Empire. As long as the followers of Christ were regarded as constituting a kind of Jewish religious sect, their acceptance was assured. But the Jews were active in denying the identification. This placed the Church in the position of being without political standing, and of having its meetings regarded as suspect. We in America have not had to face a similar situation, but, within the life-time of many of us, it has had to be faced abroad in totalitarian countries. Suppression of Christianity by the state is not an academic question but one which affects the everyday living of Christians to no small extent, calling for faith, insight, and courage.

As has been indicated, it was so when Luke wrote the Gospel that bears his name. Not only had the Jews disassociated themselves from the Christian movement, but they had also claimed that Jesus was a violator of the Roman law, a threat to the security of the Empire, and therefore deserving of death (23:2). With Domitian on the throne at Rome (the ruler referred to in the discussion of Matthew's special purpose), being a Christian was dangerous. Though the persecutions which developed consider-able proportions about the middle of the next decade had not yet begun, the prospect was terrifyingly real.

An apologetic or defense of the Christians was desperately needed, one that would face up to the political status of the followers of Christ. And Luke sought to provide it in his writing by preparing an account of the Christian movement from its humble beginning with the birth of a babe in a manger crib in an outlying province, to its arrival as a maturely defined faith at the seat of the Empire itself. He presents the life and ministry of Jesus in his Gospel and continues the narrative of the spread of the Faith and the Church in the Acts of the Apostles.

This method of telling a continuing story was far better than a formal listing of the accusations one

10

by one with a measured reply to each. For instance, when Pilate, the Roman procurator, says of Jesus, "I find no crime in this man" (23:4), and when King Herod returns him unsentenced (23: 6-12), the implications that they did not regard him as an enemy of the state are clear. And when a Roman centurion looks into the face of Jesus on the cross, and declares, "Certainly, this man was innocent!" (23:47) the Christian movement itself is being exonerated of charges of treason.

The Gospel of Luke also shows that Jesus and the disciples even prior to his death, were loyal to Rome. Centurions express open faith in him, not only on the above-mentioned occasion, but also when one of them sought healing for his slave (7:1-10).[6] In addition, our Lord supported the payment of just taxes to Caesar in return for services rendered (20: 21-25), and even attracted some tax collectors (publicans) to his cause (15:1; 19:1-10). Again, the implications of these facts as presented by Luke set the record straight in regard to the suspicions current in his day that Christians were enemies of the state.

Other individualistic emphases which are found in the Gospel According to Luke include the author's intense interest in Jesus' concern for outcasts, especially Samaritans. There was need to extend the ministry to Gentiles everywhere, not just to the Jews, the lost sheep of Israel. Luke, therefore, tells not only of the sending out of the twelve (9:1-6)

[6] Note also the considerate treatment shown to Paul by the centurion Julius, as the Apostle was en route to Rome to appeal to Caesar for justice (Acts 27:1 ff.).

on a missionary tour, but also of the dispatching of the seventy on a similar venture (10:1-12).[7] In addition, Luke takes special note of the prayer life of Jesus, his concern for the pious poor, and the place he made for women in the kingdom movement. Each of these emphases will be further considered later in this book; it is sufficient to mention them here as an indication of the individualistic character of Luke's witness to Jesus Christ.

In this chapter we have been considering the fact that the Gospels are to be read as highly personal documents. Their authors had their own faith to express as well as to report the facts in the tradition concerning Jesus. This is what makes their writings so vibrant and life-giving. Finally, we have taken a particular look at Luke's special concerns in the Gospel which bears his name and which is to be the basis of our study.

[7] It was believed at that time that there were seventy nations in the world. Luke probably saw in this gesture a symbol of the world missionary task which Matthew found in the Great Commission (Matt. 28:19-20). The two accounts of the evangelistic missions may refer to the same event; they are very similar.

The Messiah Is at Hand

THE ADVENT OF JESUS into the world provided mankind with the supreme example of selfless living. Paul never ceased to wonder at the greatness of this event and the sacrifice it entailed. Concerning it he wrote to the Corinthians, "For you know the grace of our Lord Jesus Christ, that though he was rich, yet for your sake he became poor, so that by his poverty you might become rich" (II Corinthians 8:9).

Christ Is Born

Luke the Evangelist, like Paul, was also captured by a sense of wonder concerning the cost and significance of Christ's coming. And when he wrote, compiled, and edited the Gospel that bears his name, he took special pains to express it. This is very evident in the narrative he records. It is particularly present in the songs of Mary and Zechariah. The accounts of the virgin birth of Jesus, and the birth of his forerunner, John the Baptist, include beautiful hymns of prophecy, praise, and thanksgiving. For instance, in the Magnificat, Mary sings of God's mercy in years past and of his grace in the days ahead through the advent of her son:

> "My soul magnifies the Lord,
> and my spirit rejoices in God my Savior,
> for he has regarded the low estate of his
>   handmaiden.
> For behold, henceforth all generations will
>   call me blessed;
> for he who is mighty has done great things
>   for me,
> and holy is his name.
> And his mercy is on those who fear him
> from generation to generation.
> He has shown strength with his arm,
> he has scattered the proud in the imagina-
>   tion of their hearts,
> he has put down the mighty from their
>   thrones,
> and exalted those of low degree;
> he has filled the hungry with good things,
> and the rich he has sent empty away.
> He has helped his servant Israel,
> in remembrance of his mercy,
> as he spoke to our fathers,
> to Abraham and to his posterity for ever." [1]

Luke 1:46-55

14

It was the *meaning* of Jesus' birth, and not simply the fact, that Luke sought to communicate by giving us this song of Mary.

It is the same in the psalm of Zechariah. As the forerunner of Jesus, the Baptizer is seen as a part of the new day that Christ's birth would inaugurate. The aged priest, therefore, sings of the greatness of the salvation that is to come:

"Blessed be the Lord God of Israel,
for he has visited and redeemed his people,
and has raised up a horn of salvation for us
in the house of his servant David,
as he spoke by the mouth of his holy
    prophets from of old,
that we should be saved from our enemies,
and from the hand of all who hate us;
to perform the mercy promised to our
    fathers,
and to remember his holy covenant,
the oath which he swore to our father
    Abraham, to grant us
that we, being delivered from the hand of
    our enemies,
might serve him without fear,
in holiness and righteousness before him all
    the days of our life.

[1] Some scholars conclude that these poems, as we have them, were composed by Luke and that he based them largely upon passages from the Psalms. This view, if accepted, does not in the least alter their character as testimonies to God's saving activity in history. Neither does it rule out the possibility that Mary and Zechariah expressed themselves exultantly in their high hour.

And you, child, will be called the prophet
   of the Most High;
for you will go before the Lord to prepare
   his ways,
to give knowledge of salvation to his people
in the forgiveness of their sins,
through the tender mercy of our God,
when the day shall dawn upon us from on
   high
to give light to those who sit in darkness
   and in the shadow of death,
to guide our feet into the way of peace."

Luke 1:68-79

This hymn celebrates the mercy and forgiving love of God which were drawing nigh for man's redemption. Truly, heaven is about to touch earth with gladness.

And when the holy hour of the Savior's birth arrived, Luke tells of an angelic chorus that sang:

> "Glory to God in the highest,
> and on earth peace among men
> with whom he is pleased!"
>
> Luke 2:14

Great good was in the offing; God would be glorified and peace among men would prevail.

HISTORY AND PRAISE

These hymns of faith which are found in Luke's birth narratives link history with praise. What God

16

does among men is something to sing about. As a historian, Luke sought to find the significance of history for religion, particularly in connection with the events which were related to the coming of Christ. Although the expression is cumbersome, we might call the result theologized history, that is, history viewed, interpreted, and recorded in the light of God's nature and purpose as expressed through historical events. Just as in our personal lives we may trace the pattern of Divine Providence, and know by faith that God has been leading us, so we may find the marks of his guiding hand in the occurrences of both past and present. This is what Luke did in his account of Jesus' birth. And in doing this he breathed into his record the atmosphere of pure worship.

It would be inspiring today to surround those current events in which God's purposes may be discerned with a framework of praise and thanksgiving. We greatly appreciate the free press of our nation, particularly the editorial interpretations of the news. But, although there is frequently a high sense of morality in the writings of our columnists, we find ourselves again and again looking for that fourth dimension, that God-dimension, in which the writer in his judgments, evaluations, and prognoses of the future takes into consideration the divine factors that are involved in the current scene. He who would do this must be endowed with prophetic insight. Such an appraisal of current happenings would involve a frank facing up to *all* the elements that make up the news—and history—not simply a consideration of the sequence of human motives and acts. If this were done, more of our people would put down their newspapers fortified rather than fearful of the morrow.

In the birth stories, and throughout his Gospel, Luke accomplishes what we have been suggesting. He views history and the coming of Jesus as a cosmic drama of redemption. God has bared his arm to save his people. How clearly the aged Simeon saw this when Joseph and Mary carried the young babe to Jerusalem to present him to the Lord! Luke comments that the venerable saint was inspired by the Spirit when he took the child in his arms and blessed God, saying:

> "Lord, now lettest thou thy servant depart
> in peace,
> according to thy word;
> for mine eyes have seen thy salvation
> which thou hast prepared in the presence
> of all peoples,
> a light for revelation to the Gentiles,
> and for glory to thy people Israel."
>
> Luke 2:29-32

God was acting. History was impregnated with divine love.

BACKGROUND OF DESTINY

We have been noting that Luke asserts that present and future history is at stake in God's act of sending Jesus into the world. He also indicates that our Lord himself, in pondering man's destiny, came personally to the realization that he was the Messiah.

18

His mission was to announce and make actual the kingdom of God. It is altogether likely that his understanding of his mission came gradually to Jesus as he grew up in the midst of formative influences similar to those which have surrounded growing children and youth from time immemorial—the home, the school, and the immediate neighborhood. There was also, for Jesus, the larger sphere of his own country with its religious center at Jerusalem.

Luke seems to have sensed the place of this background in Jesus' personal experience as a child and youth more fully than the other Gospel writers. He, in particular, gives us an insight into these early days in the life of our Lord. But, even so, it is only a glimpse that he provides, since he records but a single event in the period between the birth of Jesus and his baptism, when he was "about thirty years of age" (3:23). This is the account of his visit to Jerusalem when he was twelve. In addition, however, Luke inserts into the narrative a statement that is most illuminating. It suggests that during this unrecorded segment of time which has been called the "hidden years," Jesus grew and developed intellectually, physically, religiously, and socially. The passage says, "And Jesus increased in wisdom and in stature, and in favor with God and man" (2:52). Surely, here is a picture of the maturing of personality in every respect.

Writers today have sought to fill in the details of this picture as their historical imaginations have been awakened by its suggestiveness. Quite early in the life of the Church such attempts were also made.

But these were regarded finally as too speculative and unreliable. They told of clay birds which the boy Jesus modeled and which came alive, of angry words which he spoke to other boys which resulted in their death, and of magical acts by which he caused fabric materials to change their color.[2] Because these early reconstructions were not acceptable, it does not follow, however, that we must abandon our interest in the early years in the life of our Lord. Actually we have more of a basis for knowledge than at first seems to be the case.

We know that Jesus was reared in a fine Jewish home where Jehovah was revered, the Shema (Deuteronomy 6:4-5) was taught, and loving care was expressed. He probably would not have referred to God as *Father* with such strength of feeling had not Joseph been an understanding parent, and his deep love for Mary as we see her in the brief moments when she comes into the picture is a testimony to her sensitive spirit as a mother. Brothers and sisters were also very much a part of the scene in the early days, as they are in families now. There were at least four boys and two girls besides Jesus in the home (Mark 6:3). When they were grown, they did not always understand their brother (John 7:5), and it is not unlikely that this was the case when they were children, too.

Home is where the heart is, we are sometimes told, and this is pre-eminently true of a Christian home. It

[2] See "Infancy Gospels" (*The Gospel of Thomas* 1:4-10; 2:7-9; *The First Gospel of the Infancy of Jesus Christ* 15:8-15) in *The Aprocryphal New Testament* (New York: Oxford University Press, 1950), translated and edited by Montague Rhodes James.

20

may be that today we do not stay at home long enough to realize this. But in Jesus' time they did, and there was drama within the four walls with the flat roof on top. Sweeping the floor to find a lost coin (Luke 15:8-10), watching the dough rise in a bowl on the back of the oven (13:21), observing the grinding of the grain (17:35), and even washing the dishes 11:39) could be exciting.

They had their social life also, just as we do now. Sometimes they played wedding, and again it was funeral (7:31-32). When these games grew tiresome, they could hunt for birds' nests in the eaves of the house, or tramp the hills beyond Nazareth searching for fox dens (9:58). The mention of these activities has been based upon references in Luke which probably go back to Jesus' childhood experiences. Matthew carries additional notations which include fishing (Matt. 7:10), gathering wild flowers (6:28), and watching the parading caravans as they traveled the Nazareth road (Matt. 8:11).

More important than all of these, however, is the fact that at home Jesus first learned of Jehovah God. As we have noted, here he had been taught the Shema, which was the foundation of Hebrew religion. It is a trumpet call to a great faith. "Hear, O Israel: The LORD our God is one Lord; and you shall love the LORD your God with all your heart, and with all your soul, and with all your might" (Deuteronomy 6:4-5).[3] Joseph probably rehearsed Jesus in these

[3] The New Testament form of the Shema in Luke reads, "You shall love the Lord your God with all your heart, and with all your soul, and with all your strength, and with all your mind . . ." (Luke 10:27). Then Jesus added, "and your neighbor as yourself."

significant words which he was later to introduce as a part of his own teachings (Luke 10:27), adding to them the injunction to love one's neighbor as oneself (cf. Leviticus 19:18).

In my judgment, Mary also exerted a tremendous influence upon Jesus in his home. In a unique way she impressed his young life with her poetic piety. We have already referred to the Magnificat which Luke attributes to her. How moving and glorious it is! Is it too much to assume that Jesus and his mother experienced together the feeling for beauty which graced his life, as well as the devotion to the things of the Spirit which marked his ministry?

Jesus was further taught in the things of religion by the fact that his parents sent him to what was then the equivalent of our Sunday school. Only it wasn't Sunday school on the first day of the week; instead, it was a day-by-day course of instruction, where prayer, recitation of the Scriptures, and sermonic exhortation made up the curriculum. This took place, of course, at the local synagogue and the boys sat cross-legged as they vocalized their lessons reciting aloud. There was no schooling, as such, in Jesus' background, that did not involve religious education. This might suggest that when we major solely in science, literature, history, and the fine arts in the public school, we are putting religion off in a corner as of secondary importance, and divorcing it from daily living.

Before leaving the line of thought we have been pursuing, we must take note again that Luke opened

the way for such a discussion when he stated that
Jesus developed in body, mind, and spirit during
the years of childhood and youth. And we have been
attempting to suggest some of the elements which
undoubtedly were a part in his maturing. No generation can pass over lightly any one of them and be
strong.

INTIMATIONS OF A MISSION

Luke tells us quite plainly that Jesus' parents went
to Jerusalem every year to celebrate the feast of the
Passover. Many Jews did this, but not all. It suggests a regularity that indicates established religious
attitudes in which Jehovah God was worshipped and
his acts in history extolled. We cannot be certain how
many times the boy Jesus was allowed to accompany
his elders. The account of his visit at the age of
twelve may have been his very first trip to the holy
city, or it may have been one of several.

The reason that this specific celebration of the
Passover was recorded by the Evangelist, however,
was probably not because it was the first. More
likely, it was in order to give us an insight into the
growing life of the young lad, particularly in regard
to his awareness of the mission for which God had
sent him into the world. This is to be seen in Jesus'
reply to his mother when, after searching for him,
Joseph and Mary finally found him in the Temple.
In the King James Version, Jesus says, "How is it
that ye sought me? wist ye not that I must be about

my Father's business?" (2:49) The early church, as well as Luke, saw in this remark an indication of our Lord's divine calling.[4] Even though his parents did not seem to grasp its full significance at the time (2:50), the Christian community was later to do so.

We have indicated what the early church saw in the reply of Jesus to his mother. What did it mean to the twelve-year-old lad himself? Here we are left to surmise alone. It would be reasonable to assume that the full mature meaning of messiahship was not in the boy's mind at the tender age of twelve. He did feel, however, that in a very special way he belonged to the heavenly Father and that he would serve him for life. And it was this conviction that Luke wanted to lay before his readers, a conviction that deepened and enlarged until, at the Baptism, Jesus heard God say to him, "Thou art my beloved Son; with thee I am well pleased."

During the years between the early visit to the Temple and the Baptism Luke gives us no indication as to the life Jesus lived in Nazareth. If we follow his lead in the remark concerning our Lord's development, however, we may picture him as a significant member of the community, following the carpenter's trade (Mark 6:3), and devotedly attending the synagogue services. Later we are told that he went to the synagogue *as his custom was* (Luke 4:16). Tradition has it that Joseph died during this period

---

[4] If the Revised Standard Version is preferred, the reading "in my Father's house" also suggests a special mission because of the word *my*. It is intended to suggest that, in a special way, Jesus is God's Son.

and, as the oldest son, Jesus probably bore the brunt of meeting the family's financial needs.

We wish that we knew as much about Jesus' prayer practice, and his attitudes toward the religious issues of his day during these years, as we do about them throughout his ministry; but we do not. At such a time in a man's life he usually settles upon his career, builds his personal philosophy, and discovers the girl he is to marry, or actually marries. These are the significant decisions which determine his future, and Jesus must have faced them along with his brothers in the flesh.

A Call and a Response

It was at the Baptism that Jesus' great call came, even though, as we have seen, there were probably intimations of it before. Unlike Mark, Luke lays the background for this epochal event, for that it surely was, by giving us a rather detailed account of John the Baptist's revival (3:1-20). This rugged preacher proclaimed the near advent of the Day of the Lord which was to bring God's judging of the wicked, his blessing of the faithful, and his sending of the Messiah. Great crowds responded, including both the Jewish hierarchy and the common people. Such moral seriousness had not been known among the Jews since the days of the prophets. There was an immediacy to the stern preacher's summons to a baptism of repentance that pierced to the marrow of the soul. He also insisted upon restoring right relations with the needy and the poor, and a putting away of sham and pretense among the pious.

There was something in this religious movement that commandeered Jesus' attention. I use this word in an attempt to suggest the force of the appeal which the awakening had for him. It was so great that he left Nazareth and made the long trek to the South Jordan Valley to see, to hear, to wonder—and to respond.

Luke does not provide as much detail in describing the actual baptism of Jesus as does Matthew. While the latter records a conversation between Jesus and John, in which the prophet expresses his unworthiness to baptize the Messiah, Luke simply states the fact that John baptized him. Matthew's account was probably written to reassure those who were troubled because Jesus submitted to baptism at the hands of another. Not only was John a lesser personage than the Master, but his baptism was unto repentance for the remission of sins. And Jesus was without sin!

These facts were evidently not a problem for Luke and his readers. He regarded Jesus' baptism as his response to God's call, and as his dedication to the Kingdom John was announcing. Our Lord was not repenting for sin, but was taking his stand with John and the people in a movement of deep moral and spiritual significance. And in this high hour, God summoned him to his mission as the Messiah, and anointed him with the Holy Spirit to empower him for the fulfillment of his destiny.

A call, a response, an empowerment—these three belong together in the economy of God's relation to those he summons. This pattern, if we may refer to it as such, held true not only for our Lord; it has also been God's way throughout the centuries. And it applies not only to the great and near great, but also to every person who would become a follower of Christ in doing the will of God.

III

Jesus and
His Temptations══════

THE SYNOPTIC GOSPELS agree that following
the high call to messiahship which Jesus experienced
at his baptism there was a period of terrific temptation. They agree also that he emerged from these days
as victor. These temptations are regarded as genuine,
for Jesus is presented as possessing real freedom of
choice. He *could* have chosen to walk a different
road than that which the heavenly Father willed—
he could have, *but didn't*. This fact gives significance
to his sinlessness. It was not just the absence of sin;
instead, it was the presence of an unbroken align-
ment with the will of almighty God. This is positive.
This is real.

We shall not understand Luke's portrait of Christ
unless we begin here. This positive sinlessness is

illustrated not only by the temptations of our Lord at the outset of his ministry, but also by the decisions that he made in subsequent days. Throughout his lifetime he was tempted. For instance, Luke alone says that at the close of the forty days in the wilderness, the devil "departed from him until an opportune time" (4:13). It was not over, ended, quits; it was just beginning. And at the Last Supper, when Jesus' earthly ministry was drawing to a close, our evangelist records that he said to his disciples, "Ye are they which have continued with me in my temptations" (22:28. K.J.V.).

Before we look at the wilderness temptations which Jesus faced, and which Luke records, we should take note of the fact that the greater the power or potential in a person's life, the more tremendous will be the temptations. Take Jesus of Nazareth, for example; take the divine power which he felt within himself, the personal force of his being, and the strength of his mind and body. The possession of these qualities placed our Lord in situation after situation where the tides of temptation swirled about him in a mighty swell, and he was shaken to the depths of his being.

Luke 4:1-13, along with Matthew 4:1-11, gives marked attention to the forty days of temptation Jesus spent in the wilderness, before beginning his public ministry as the Messiah. Mark merely mentions it in two brief verses (1:12-13). Its importance loomed larger in the thinking of the early church with the passing of time, however, and this called for a fuller consideration. It is probable that Luke and Matthew found the data for their accounts in an earlier writing which scholars refer to as "Q," the first letter of the German word *Quelle,* meaning "source." Possibly this may have been written originally in Aramaic at Syrian Antioch about the year A.D. 50.[1] The final source for the information of what took place during these days, however, must have been Jesus himself. He was alone at this time of temptation and only he could have revealed what took place.

In all probability Jesus shared this tremendous experience with the disciples when it would have helped them most. Since, as we have already seen, Luke tells us that Jesus referred to the temptations which beset him throughout his ministry at the Last Supper, this could have been an appropriate occasion for revealing his own struggle. We know that, in the death that he was to face on the morrow, the conception of messiahship which he held was at issue, even as it was during the forty days in the wilderness when he was making his plans for the future. What he had decided upon then (and how long ago it must have seemed!) was now to come to its tragic, and yet glorious, fruition in the cross.

[1] This is Streeter's conclusion. It is also held by Moffatt if "Q" is identified with the Matthewan Logia. Others regard it as a Greek document because of linguistic factors evident in Matthew's and Luke's use of it. See Alfred M. Perry, *The Interpreter's Bible,* VII, p. 64.

Background Considerations

We should take note of certain significant references in Luke's account of these matters, by way of background, before turning to the actual temptations themselves. First of all, he says that Jesus was "led by the Spirit" during this period in his life. It was the same Spirit that came upon him at the Baptism. Mark had made this even more explicit by indicating that "the Spirit immediately [after the Baptism] drove him [Jesus] out into the wilderness." Like Luke, he wanted his readers to see that there was a connection between the two events. The Temptations follow the Baptism as the night the day.

The wilderness provided a stark and desolate setting for the temptations of Jesus. It was a section thirty-five by fifteen miles between the central plateau of Judea and the Dead Sea. Bare rocks of limestone, crevasses between precipices that rose 1,200 feet high and smoothed out as they approached the sea, gave a severity to the landscape that matched the struggle in our Lord's soul. Sour soil, burnt-out hillsides, and jungle growth were characteristic of the region; intense heat by day and cold by night added further to its severity. Fierce beasts frequented the area, particularly lions, wolves, leopards, and wild boar. There was no comfort in such a site. Little wonder, then, that Mark states (Luke does not carry this word) that the angels ministered to Jesus during this time of temptation.

Another point to consider is that the space of time

mentioned, forty days, should probably not be taken too literally. It was a figure that stood for a considerable period of time, as in the reference to the forty years of wilderness wandering for the Jews, and the forty days and forty nights of rain which fell in the time of Noah.

Brief consideration should also be given to the statement of Luke that Jesus "ate nothing in those days." Mark makes no reference to this, and Matthew refers only to the fact that Jesus fasted for forty days, leaving the way open to conclude that he probably ate something, however little it may have been. Among the Jews fasting was required by the Law only on the Day of Atonement. The Pharisees, however, urged orthodox Jews to abstain from food often, and themselves fasted usually on Monday and Thursday. Later, Jesus was to say that there was a time for fasting and a time not to fast (Luke 5:33-39). It all depended upon the needs of the spirit, as over against the demands of the body. There were times when food was of quite secondary importance. It was thus in the wilderness of temptation.

The last of these background references has to do with the portrayal of Jesus' experience itself at the hands of Luke. He uses pictorial language, by which spiritual and subjective matters are given an external semblance which they probably did not originally possess. It is doubtful whether a photographic record of the scene would have shown the image of a personal devil, or pictured Jesus actually being carried to the pinnacle of the Temple. And as for the temptations themselves, turning stones into bread, jumping from the Temple, and bowing in worship before the devil, all mean more than doing just these physical things. They have a far deeper import than is implied by the actions they first call to mind. Actually, they represent certain procedures which Jesus was tempted to follow in the accomplishment of his messianic mission.[2] The account is highly symbolical and probably owes its form to the way in which Jesus originally reported his experience. He who spoke consistently in parables, and made such eloquent use of metaphors, did so here also, as he described the storm in his soul with such awesome vividness.

The Temptations

STONES INTO BREAD

Paul Tillich, the distinguished contemporary theologian, customarily uses the word "possibility" for temptation. This is particularly valuable in helping us to understand the temptations of Jesus in the wilderness. Our Lord was here confronted with several possible courses of action or patterns for messiahship. The questions he faced he decided on the basis of the will of the heavenly Father as he saw it. There was something in each of the "possibilities" which made its appeal—at least temporarily —and for this reason each offered a genuine temptation, not a synthetic suggestion. In some cases the proposed course of action even seemed to be undergirded by Scripture, at least there was a traditional bias in its favor. In other cases it seemed to be supported by the contemporary public opinion of Jesus' own day, so that quick success appeared likely to attend it. And, as the Messiah, Jesus wanted to succeed. Make no mistake about it.

The Baptism had brought to Jesus a call to messiahship and an empowerment by the Spirit to fulfill it. Fresh from the ecstasy of this high hour, he had gone into the wilderness to face its implications. When the tempter said to him, "If thou be the Son of God . . . ," [*] our Lord was being asked to doubt the voice which he had heard at his baptism, saying "Thou art my beloved Son; with thee I am well pleased." If! If! If!

Many a Christian has faced the same temptation following his conversion. Was it real? Was it only self-hypnotism or the result of group suggestion? Was its origin in a guilt complex which had been repressed into the subconscious, or was it a valid spiritual experience? These, and many other ideas, come into our minds under such circumstances.

By way of answer, Jesus was tempted to produce a physical miracle—to turn stones into bread. He was tempted to do so—but he did not. Although one needs always to be both reflective and objective regarding his own religious experiences, the temptation to prove their genuineness by material devices is utterly misleading. A spiritual truth can only be

[2] See the author's *The Life and Teachings of Jesus* (Nashville: Abingdon Press, 1955), p. 180. Chapter 9 provides helpful background reading on the Temptations.

[*] King James Version.

authenticated in spiritual terms. We do not attempt to prove that a picture is beautiful by the use of a caliper or slide rule. Although geometric proportion may aid the composition of a painting, its aesthetic value cannot be measured by geometry. The production of physical phenomena is no guarantee of spiritual power. Jesus might have turned stones into bread, but this would not have proved the genuineness of his Father's voice at his baptism. It would only have indicated that he could turn stones into bread, and nothing more.

There is another aspect of the first temptation which should be considered. It carried with it the suggestion that Jesus as the Messiah should become an economic liberator, that by producing food for the body he should win people for the kingdom of God. The ancient Jewish fathers had long since dreamed of a land flowing with milk and honey, and the rule of the messianic king was expected to be a time of plenty. That the Jews needed food now was obvious, and that they would follow one who provided it was equally clear. But where would such a program lead? Might it not serve more immediate ends to the neglect or defeat of the Messiah's ultimate purpose? Was bringing men food tantamount to bringing them God? The answer to these questions came to Jesus, in part, through his knowledge of the Scriptures. He recalled that it was written,

> "Man does not live by bread alone"
>> Deuteronomy 8:3

This was it!

Note that the above quotation does not say that man does not live by bread *at all*. Instead, it clearly states that man does not live by bread *alone*, implying that he is more than a body. He needs beauty as well as bread, God as well as goods. The rest of the quotation from Deuteronomy which Luke does not give, but which Matthew does in somewhat different words, adds "but that man lives by everything that proceeds out of the mouth of the Lord." The Word of God is bread too. And the truth of the matter is that if men find God, there will be the disposition in their hearts to share their material bread with all, so that none shall be hungry. In the modern world, our basic problem is not the production of bread, but its just distribution. And here God has a Word to speak, if the world will but listen. God first; bread second; enough for all; this is the divine sequence.

Worship Me

Luke's order of the Temptations differs from Matthew's. There is no way to tell which is the more historical. Actually, the variations are not significant since the three temptations recorded are identical and their main points do not lie in their sequence. I have always preferred Matthew's arrangement on psychological grounds. It is cumulative and mounts to a terrific climax in the final temptation. His order is (1) turning stones into bread, (2) leaping from the Temple, and (3) bowing down in worship before the devil. Luke, on the other hand, lists them as

(1) turning stones into bread, (2) bowing down in worship before the devil, and (3) leaping from the Temple. We are, of course, following Luke in this study.

The temptation to worship Satan is usually thought to be a suggestion to use the ways of the world to win the world, to employ such methods as violence, force, intimidation, and compromise. Rome had employed these to the full, and on every hand seemed to be a ranking success. Her eagles screamed loudly from countless banners. Here was proof of their effectiveness. But the kingdom of God was not to be a material realm. Righteousness was its law, love its ruling principle. To force men into goodness was not morally sound, and to support violence, intimidation, and compromise on the ground that the end justified the means was suicidal.

It was the political aspect of this temptation that had the biggest tug. For centuries past, certainly since Isaiah (Isa. 9:6-7; 11:1-10), the ideal of the Kingdom as an earthly empire had been in the thinking of the Jews. It was still the dominant outlook. There was a sect among them, the Zealots, which advocated revolutionary action against Rome to bring about this desired end. Jesus was later to select a disciple from this group in the person of Simon the Zealot. But we can be sure that this follower's thinking changed considerably in the company of the Master.

It was the Scriptures, again, which came to Jesus in this time of need with a divine word of guidance.

The Law as laid down in Deuteronomy 6:13 had insisted that obedience to God rather than to men was the rule of righteous living. Jesus saw clearly that God's way was not the way of the devil, or to be more specific, that it was contrary to the way of the world. Therefore, he said:

> "It is written,
> 'You shall worship the Lord your God
> and him only shall you serve.'"
>
> Luke 4:8

The words of the devil to Jesus in this temptation, when he claimed that the authority and the glory of the kingdoms of the world belonged to him, reflected a current belief among the Jews that the world was under the temporary control of the devil and his angels. The Christian Church was to assert later that by his death Jesus had broken this enslaving grip, and that all who were "in Christ" were free from the devil's power.

LEAP FROM THE TEMPLE

According to Luke's order, the last of the three wilderness temptations was the suggestion that Jesus leap from the pinnacle of the Temple, assured that he would land unharmed four hundred and fifty feet below in the Kedron Valley. Had not God promised man protection against natural calamity, so that he would not dash his foot against a stone? (4:11)[3]

[3] See Psalm 91:11-12.

As we have said previously, this probably was not a temptation to perform this particular act literally. Rather, it was a suggestion that Jesus use the methods of sensationalism as a shortcut to winning a following for the Kingdom he was to proclaim. Spectacular events were expected when the Messiah came. The apocalyptists had used highly symbolical language to foretell the visitation of God in judgment at the end of time.[4] Even the Qumran community of the Dead Sea Scrolls had its apocalyptic writing.[5] The times were ripe for a miracle-working messiah. Why should not Jesus be just this?

It was a good question and, in view of the fact that Jesus later performed mighty acts of healing which attracted great crowds, we may conclude that he gave the matter considerable thought. The problem here, which Jesus found to be very real as his ministry developed, is that men will follow quickly and eagerly when confronted with a spectacle. But they will just as readily tire of it, and turn elsewhere for new excitement. Miraculous feats indicate little concerning the character of God as holy love. They do not lead men to repentance and personal renewal.

Leaping from the Temple was no less than putting God to a test. He must intervene to save—or else!

[4] Apocalypticism is the view that the end of the age will be attended by signs and wonders, with dramatic interventions by God from on high. Cf. Daniel 7:13-14; I Enoch 46:3-4; 48:3; 62:5, 14.

[5] See "The War of the Sons of Light with the Sons of Darkness" in Millar Burrows' *The Dead Sea Scrolls* (New York: The Viking Press, 1955), pp. 390-399.

This was not the way of trust and faith. And therefore, Jesus said to the devil,

"You shall not tempt the Lord your God . . ."
Luke 4:12

This is what the Jews had done at Massah when they sought to get God to show them his presence on their own terms (Deuteronomy 6:16). Our Lord would have none of it.

We have seen that temptation for Jesus was very real. It was related to his personal life situation as he sought to discover and follow the will of his heavenly Father in an evil world. Because of the intensity of his vision and the depth of his dedication, the temptations he faced were on a plane above that which others knew, above and more awesome. And yet, they were not unlike those which every person faces in relation to the issues of his own life.

IV

Jesus and the Scriptures

THE OLD TESTAMENT became the Scripture of Christians in the early church, just as it had been Jesus' Bible also. It continued to nourish their faith through its moving passages, as it had inspired the belief of Israel in one God before the advent of the Messiah. And Luke, no exception to the rule, also drew inspiration from the sacred pages, though not in just the same way as the other evangelists.

Sometimes the authors of the Gospels will make an editorial remark which reveals their attitude toward Scripture. Matthew does this frequently. He customarily views the events in the life of Jesus as the fulfillment of prophecy. The virgin birth (1:23), the flight into Egypt (2:15), the slaughter by Herod of the innocent babes (2:17), the moving of Joseph

43

and Mary to Nazareth in order to rear Jesus there (2:23), the preaching of John the Baptist (3:3), Jesus' departure from Nazareth after the arrest of John (4:13, 16), his urging the healed not to make him known (12:16 f.), his reason for speaking in parables (13:14 f., 34 f.), and the Triumphal Entry (21:4)—all these Matthew specifically records as occurring in order to fulfill the Scriptures.

By way of contrast, there is practically no reference to the fulfillment of prophecy in Luke's editorial comments, even when he is reporting the same event as Matthew. This has sometimes led to the assumption that Luke, the Gentile Christian, did not have the same appreciation of the Hebrew Scriptures as did Matthew the Jew. This need not be true. The absence of these references to the fulfillment of prophecy in his editing may mean only that this particular aspect of the sacred writings was not uppermost in his thinking. Actually, there is more of a reflection of the beauty of the Old Testament in Luke than in Matthew. When we turn to the birth stories and read the hymns of Elizabeth, Mary, and Zechariah we can see that this is the case. They are almost a mosaic of scriptural passages.

The presence of these songs in Luke's stories of Jesus' birth indicates that he appreciated the Old Testament. First of all, he took care to record them. Secondly, there is the possibility that, if he did not actually compose them, the mark of his own poetic sensitivity is upon them. And in the third place, the same feeling for the Old Testament which Luke's writing in his Gospel indicates is even more marked in the Acts of the Apostles, which he also wrote. There is but little room to doubt that Luke revered the Scriptures along with other early Christians.

A New Interpretation

Not only did Luke appreciate the Scriptures himself; he also was sensitive to what they meant to Jesus. On this point all of the Gospel writers join in the same insight. By this time only the Law and the Prophets had been canonized, but the other writings were also being recognized as possessing more than passing authority. Luke reports Jesus as saying, "It is easier for heaven and earth to pass away, than for one dot of the law to become void" (16:17).[1] Even in the face of the preaching of the good news of the kingdom of God, the Law held firm. Luke believed this also. Possibly he was convinced that to follow Jesus was to fulfill the Law. Certainly its intent and spirit were being realized.

Before looking at certain specific instances which illustrate Jesus' attitude toward the Scriptures, some general notations are in order. We shall discover that in our Lord's use of his Bible he was not a literalist. It was not what was written *but what was meant* that counted most. On occasion, he preferred one passage as over against another. For instance,

[1] The dot (tittle) probably represented either the small stroke added to a letter to distinguish it from another which would otherwise be the same, or the "horns, thorns, and crowns" which were decorative apexes placed above certain letters in scrolls of the Torah.

Genesis 1:27 and 2:24 (cf. Mark 10:2-9) seemed to him more significant in relation to divorce than Deuteronomy 24:1-4, which the Pharisees quoted. He who was Lord of the Sabbath was also Lord of the sacred writings. This is seen particularly when he places his own judgment above that of earlier biblical authors. The familiar "You have heard that it was said to the men of old," followed by "But I say to you" is a clear indication that he did his own thinking when he read the Scriptures.[2]

Not only did Jesus interpret his Bible as one who had authority in this area, he also favored certain sections of it—even as we do today—as evidenced by our own practice of reading particular passages and neglecting others. And it is interesting to realize that his favorite books are ours also. In the order of the frequency of the references to them they were Isaiah, Deuteronomy, Psalms, Leviticus, Hosea, Zechariah, Genesis, Exodus, Daniel, First Samuel, Numbers, Nehemiah, and Jeremiah. In this connection, also, it should be mentioned that he seemed to go along with the views of his time regarding biblical authorship. For instance, Moses had written the Law, and David had composed the Psalms.

There is yet another aspect of Jesus' use of the Scriptures which should be mentioned in this general review. Certain Old Testament characters made a more profound impression upon him than did others. At least, the fact that he made reference to them

[2] Compare Matthew 5:21-48 for several instances of this approach in relation to former teaching regarding killing, adultery, divorce, oath-taking, retaliation, and hatred of enemies.

rather than to others would seem to lead to this conclusion. And once again, these turn out to be our favorites, too. Here they are: Abel, Abraham, Isaac, Jacob, Moses, Noah, Jonah, Lot and his wife, David, Solomon, the queen of Sheba, Elijah, Elisha, the widow of Zarephath, and Naaman. What a list! They represent the colorful figures of the Scriptures, those who possessed imagination and daring. They were not always exemplary in what they did, but they were always vibrant personalities. No one could accuse them of being dull. Certainly they caught Jesus' attention out of the distant past, and by mentioning them he enabled them to contribute to his own day—and also to ours.

Selected Specific Situations in Which Jesus Used His Bible

When we examine the specific situations that Luke records in which Jesus, directly or indirectly, used his Bible we discover that he employed it in at least four ways. First, he turned to it in making the most important decisions of his career.[3] Next, he had occasion to refer to it in his preaching.[4] Again, he quoted from it in relation to certain public acts he performed.[5] And finally, his Bible was helpful to him in situations when he was reflecting upon the

[3] Luke 4:1-13, 16-30; 9:18-36.
[4] Luke 7:27; 11:29 f.; 13:28 f.; 17:25 f.; 20:27 f.; 20:41 f.
[5] Luke 6:3; 19:28; 19:46.

47

events of the day, particularly when they bore a reference to himself.[6]

THE TEMPTATIONS *Luke 4:1-13*

We have seen already that Jesus turned to the Scriptures during the wilderness days of temptation.[7] At this point, let us consider *how* he read them under these circumstances. In the suggestion that he turn stones into bread and become a bread-giving messiah, an economic liberator, Jesus found guidance in a passage from Deuteronomy. It would be truer to say that he discovered wisdom in the situation behind the passage, rather than in the words themselves.

This is an important difference. Our Lord was not quoting biblical verses, but was discerning biblical truth and applying it to the situation he was facing. During the wilderness days under Moses the people were looking for material blessings in the inheritance of the promised land. The author of Deuteronomy saw that this was where they erred; God and his word was the true treasure: ". . . man does not live by bread alone, but . . . man lives by everything that proceeds out of the mouth of the LORD" (8:3). Here was a great teaching that was applicable to Jesus' decision concerning the method and message of the Kingdom. God came first; bread would follow.

In the second temptation (Luke's order) to bow

[6] Luke 20:9 ff.; 24:25; 24:44.
[7] See pp. 36-41.

down before the devil, meaning to use the ways of the world to win the world, Jesus again found wisdom in the experience of the past as it was reflected in the Scriptures. As before, it was a word from Deuteronomy which came home to him with such great force. Here it was insisted that obedience to Jehovah was the true source of righteousness. This meant to be wholly loyal; there could be no compromise. By being faithful, had not Israel been delivered out of Egypt? And by being faithful now—in Jesus' day—there would be deliverance again: "You shall fear the LORD your God; you shall serve him, and swear by his name" (Deuteronomy 6:13).

The temptation to make a leap from the Temple, in the expectation that angels would save him, and that he would thus draw a large crowd of curious spectators, was even more subtle than the other two temptations. On the surface, such action seemed to be justified by Scripture. But Jesus soon realized that it would have been contrary to the will of God, that it would, in fact, be "tempting God"! It was recorded, in Deuteronomy again, that at Massah the people had urged God to make himself known to them, but to do so on their own terms. This was dictating to God, no less. And to leap from the Temple would be the same kind of dictation. It would be testing God; he would be compelled to intervene or Jesus would be killed. This was not faith, such faith as belonged to the Kingdom: "You shall not put the LORD your God to the test as you tested him at Massah" (Deuteronomy 6:16). In all three temptations the biblical situation spoke to

Jesus in his personal situation, and the divine word of guidance proved helpful.

The Nazareth Sermon *Luke 4:16-30*

Luke placed the account of the visit of Jesus to Nazareth, where he preached in the synagogue, directly following the Temptations, even though it clearly suggests that a considerable ministry had already occurred. The reason he did this, I think, was because he found here a description of the type of messiah Jesus had decided to be. In the wilderness our Lord had rejected certain methods. But what did he select in their place? The Nazareth sermon provides the answer.

The passage from Isaiah (61:1-2)[8] which Jesus read on this occasion may have been the regular reading for the day. Again, our Lord could have selected it because of its description of the Servant upon whom the Spirit of Jehovah was sent and who performed such gracious service. In any case, he applied it to himself.[9]

> "The Spirit of the Lord is upon me,
> because he has anointed me to preach
> good news to the poor.

[8] This passage is taken from the Septuagint text of Isaiah 61:1-2. The words, "To set at liberty those who are oppressed" came from the Septuagint of Isaiah 58:6.

[9] Some scholars hold that the early church, not our Lord himself, applied this passage to Jesus. If this is the case, it would still indicate that the early Christians were convinced that Jesus identified himself with the "anointed" one described in this passage.

He has sent me to proclaim release to the
    captives
and recovering of sight to the blind,
to set at liberty those who are oppressed,
to proclaim the acceptable year of the
    Lord." Luke 4:18-19

This was to be Jesus' kind of messiah; this was to
be his program. The Scriptures had spelled it out.
As God's servant he would help the needy, deliver
the oppressed, and serve the pious poor; not an
economic administrator, not a wonder worker, not an
earthly ruler, but a Prophetic Servant. Naturally,
this would not please the Jews who were expecting a
messiah far more glamorous and lordly. And Luke
wants us to see in the negative reaction of the people
in the synagogue to Jesus' announcement on this occasion, a presentiment of the cross itself, as they
sought to cast him over the brow of the hill.

A Sabbath Observance *Luke 6:1-5*

With the passing of time Jesus' ministry ran a
rugged course. At first there were the crowds and
the days of popularity. As Jesus' prophetic message
began to sink deep into their consciousness, however,
there developed animosities against him and it. The
religious leaders resented the authority he assumed,
particularly in regard to the observance of the
Sabbath.

Some of the regulations for this holy day that they
insisted upon as basic, Jesus regarded as inhuman

51

and limiting. Such restrictions as the forbidding of healing, the pedantic interpretation of certain acts of human welfare as "labor," and the multiple special case legislations by which the simpler sabbath laws had been made unbelievably complicated (Exodus 20:8-11; 31:12-17; Deuteronomy 5:12-15)—such restrictions were unbearable to Jesus, even as they were burdensome to the people themselves.[10]

It was in relation to one of these restrictions that Jesus had occasion to refer to the Scriptures, and this is our reason for considering it here. Our Lord and his disciples were walking through the grain-fields on a certain Sabbath. Some of them had plucked the ripe ears of grain and, after rubbing away the hulls, had eaten them. The Pharisees took issue and accused them of breaking the Sabbath law. According to the rabbis, there were two sins in this act. Plucking the ears was regarded as reaping, and rubbing them, as threshing. Both were forbidden on the Sabbath.

The issue here, as Jesus saw it, was the Law versus human need. It is not likely that the disciples would have starved or actually suffered without the grain. But the objections of the Pharisees involved a principle which applied all down the line in regard to Sabbath regulations. Which came first, persons or the Law? Persons, of course! The Scriptures made this abundantly clear. Had not David, the prototype of the Messiah himself, allowed his men who were in dire need of food to eat the bread of the Presence,

[10] For a fuller consideration of these matters see the author's *The Life and Teachings of Jesus,* p. 228 and following.

permitted only to the priests? Indeed he had (I Samuel 21)! Just so, "The sabbath was made for man, not man for the sabbath; so the Son of man is lord even of the sabbath" (Mark 2:27-28). Luke quotes only the latter part of this statement, where Jesus is referred to as the Son of man who is lord of the Sabbath. It is his tribute to the supremacy of Jesus as Lord over all lesser institutions, even the Sabbath itself.

Again, in this reference to David, Jesus is not using the Scriptures as a proof-text. It is the principle involved that counts. David is not to be copied; rather, his spirit is to be followed.

Some Warnings *Luke 11:29-32; 13:28; 17:26-32*

The use of the Scriptures in preaching was a regular practice in Jesus' day. It was customary at the synagogue service to read from the Law, and sometimes from the Prophets, in Hebrew. In Palestine this was translated into Aramaic, and a sermon of sorts based upon the passage was then delivered. This is what Jesus did at Nazareth when he read from Isaiah, and then applied the passage to himself and his work as the Messiah.

Our Lord used the Scriptures in his preaching outside the synagogue also. It was quite an informal procedure, consisting of references to persons or events in Israel's past which illustrated his point— informal but highly effective, particularly in relation to warnings against sin and its results. Three such instances are listed at the beginning of this section.

In the first case (Luke 11:29-32), Jesus criticized the people for demanding a sign, such as temple-jumping, perhaps. Only the sign of Jonah, which Luke interpreted as a voice raised to call men to repentance, would be given.[11] Then our Lord told the people that both the queen of Sheba and the men of Nineveh would shame them at the Judgment, because she and they had shown faith, even without the presence of the Son to inspire them.

On another occasion (Luke 13:28), in a similar vein, Jesus represented Abraham, Isaac, Jacob, and all the prophets as enjoying the blessings of the kingdom of God. They had been men of high belief, even though they lived in the distant past, while those in the present hour of God's visitation were doubters. The Judgment would show clearly which were right.

Finally, at another time,[12] Luke records Jesus as referring to the sudden coming of the Judgment. He compared this hour to the destructive flood in the days of Noah, and to the fire and brimstone which consumed Sodom and its people, and to the doom which overtook Lot's wife (Luke 17:26-32). In both instances the people were completely surprised; instead, they should have been ready. There was great persuasion in these examples from the

[11] In Matthew the sign is said to consist in the fact that just as Jonah was three days and nights inside the whale, so Jesus would be a similar time in the heart of the earth (Matthew 12:40).

[12] Matthew places this teaching of Jesus in the apocalyptic discourse (chapter 24), where it is also quite appropriate. Jesus may have used the same biblical illustrations on numerous occasions, even as public speakers do today.

Scriptures. The sacred writings spoke with spiritual authority, even as they do today.

AT CAESAREA PHILIPPI *Luke 9:18-27*

Thus far in this chapter we have seen how Jesus used his Bible in the wilderness of temptation, at Nazareth when identifying himself with the Servant-Messiah of Isaiah 61, in a situation when he came into conflict with the Pharisees regarding Sabbath observances, and in preaching as he warned the people of the impending Judgment. We shall now take a look at another situation which Luke records, and in which it is a likely conclusion that Jesus also turned to the Scriptures.

The reason I have said that it is a likely conclusion, instead of stating that it is an indisputable fact, is that Jesus does not openly refer to the Scriptures at this point. But this need not mean that they were not in his thinking at the time. Actually, the ideas our Lord expresses on this occasion are so grounded in the suffering servant conception of Isaiah 53 that it is all but inevitable to conclude that he had this Scripture in mind. This is further confirmed by the fact that Luke records that the early church later interpreted the cross in terms of this same suffering servant ideal (Acts 8:26-40). Had they not taken this view from Jesus himself?

We have already considered two instances in which enmity against Jesus had developed, at Nazareth where the people rose up against him, and on the Sabbath when the Pharisees criticized him. It is clear in the Gospels that this kind of reaction continued, becoming more virulent with the passing of time. What did this presage for the future? Would God's Messiah be rejected by his own people? This possiblility was not in the popular mind, but it was probably present in our Lord's. Where to turn?

In the next chapter we shall see how prayer helped Jesus in this hour of decision. Here it is his use of the Scriptures that concerns us. In Second Isaiah (53:3-5), the prophet, writing in the midst of the sorrows of exile, was inspired by God to envision a redemption that would come through suffering. This is what he wrote:

> He was despised and rejected by men;
>   a man of sorrows, and acquainted with
>   grief;
> and as one from whom men hide their faces
>   he was despised, and we esteemed him
>   not.
>
> Surely he has borne our griefs
>   and carried our sorrows;
> yet we esteemed him stricken,
>   smitten by God, and afflicted.
> But he was wounded for our transgressions,
>   he was bruised for our iniquities;
> upon him was the chastisement that made
>   us whole,
>   and with his stripes we are healed.

The author of these words probably had before him a picture of the nation Israel, at least the spiritual

56

core of it, as fulfilling a particular destiny by becoming a fellowship of sufferers who would, in love, bear the brunt of the sins of others. But could it not apply to an individual just as well?

This conception of the messianic destiny of the Jews had been largely passed over through the centuries, and in Jesus' day it was not regarded seriously. But there was true wisdom here. In the light of the actual persecution our Lord was facing, and the prospect of its increasing, did not these words suggest to him a profound principle of interpretation? And in this sense were they not a kind of prophecy of the cross? Was it not, in part at least, through this Scripture that Jesus concluded he was to be a suffering Messiah?

The answer to these questions seems to me to be affirmative. Once again Jesus' Bible had contained the inspiration and insight that had a direct bearing upon his life and the decision—the awe-full decision —he had to make. Turning to the disciples he said: "The Son of man must suffer many things, and be rejected by the elders and chief priests and scribes, and be killed, and on the third day be raised" (Luke 9:22).

If space permitted, still other instances of our Lord's use of the Scriptures as reported in Luke could be cited and interpreted. These would include Jesus' reference to his death at Jerusalem (18:31 ff.), the triumphal entry (19:28 ff.), the cleansing of the Temple (19:45 f.), the parable of the vineyard (20:9 ff.), the teaching on divorce (20:27 ff.), and the reference to the Messiah as David's son (20:41). There are additional illustrations in the other Gospels which Luke does not mention. Deeply moving among these are the words spoken by our Lord from the cross itself (Matthew 27:46).

If our Bibles meant as much to us as Jesus' Scriptures meant to him, we would find in them what our fathers aptly called "wisdom unto salvation." John Wesley is an illustration of how these Scriptures can awaken a new spiritual and devotional life within us. On the day of his conversion he read the Bible in the morning, heard it read at St. Paul's Cathedral in the afternoon, and that night he listened to the reading of Luther's preface to the Epistle to the Romans. Wesley averaged fifteen sermons a week, traveled 5,000 miles a year on horseback, and the Bible went with him. It was the same with his traveling preachers. From the first, Methodism has been a Bible-reading movement, and it remains so to this very day.

C H A P T E R V

Prayer in the
Life of Christ════════

JESUS' PRAYER LIFE WAS AN OUTGROWTH of his personal faith in the heavenly Father. Let us not miss this point. He prayed because he believed in God; and because he believed in God, he prayed. This means that his praying was genuinely personal and very real. Although he is our Great Example here as elsewhere, he did not pray just to provide an example. Instead, he prayed because he needed to, wanted to, and loved to pray. Prayer made a difference in his career as the Messiah. The Gospels indicate this with abundant clarity.

The Gospel of Luke in particular should be known as the New Testament writing that majors in prayer. There are more references to praying in this book than in any other single composition of the early church, including the Epistles of Paul. All in all, Luke gives us fifteen instances of Jesus' prayer life and of his teachings on this theme. Ten of these depict Jesus in the very act of praying.[1] And five present his remarks concerning prayer.[2] Of the fifteen, seven are reported in Luke alone;[3] five are found in one or more of the other Gospels, but only Luke states definitely that on the occasion mentioned Jesus was praying, or records the prayer he made.[4] One teaching statement is given in Luke and Matthew only.[5] All three of the Synoptic Gospels mention but two of Luke's references.[6] From this brief recital it can be seen that Luke was particularly sensitive to prayer and praying. The Third Evangelist seems to have gone out of his way to highlight this aspect of the life of devotion in the ministry of our Lord.

A listing of the situations in which Luke takes note that Jesus prayed is most revealing. These were: 1. at the time of his baptism (3:21); 2. when the multitudes pressed upon him (5:16); 3. before calling the Twelve (6:12); 4. at the feeding of the five thousand (9:16); 5. on the Mount of Transfiguration (9:29 ff.); 6. upon the return of the seventy from their evangelistic mission (10:21 f.); 7. when giving the Lord's Prayer (11:1 ff.); 8. when praying for Peter (22:31 f.); 9. in the Garden of Gethsemane (22:41, 44) and from the cross (23:46). These were

[1] Luke 3:21; 5:16; 6:12; 9:16; 9:29 ff.; 10:21 f.; 11:1; 22:31 f.; 22:41, 44; 23:46. Luke 4:42 assumes that Jesus was praying, although it does not expressly state it.
[2] Luke 11:5 ff.; 11:9 ff.; 18:1 ff.; 18:9 f.; 22:40.
[3] Luke 10:21 f.; 11:5 ff.; 18:1 ff.; 18:9 f.; 22:31 f.; 22:40; 23:46.
[4] Luke 3:21; 5:16; 6:12; 9:29 ff.; 11:1.
[5] Luke 11:9.
[6] Luke 9:16; 22:41, 44.

the crisis hours of his life when decisions of eternal consequence had to be made. Each was an hour of high issue. And prayer made the difference between light and darkness.

From these experiences in praying, Luke makes it clear that Jesus emerged with a new sense of direction. He had come face to face with his heavenly Father, and in this encounter had found wisdom and strength to move forward. We can feel quite confident that Luke believed that prayer was a deciding factor in the life of his Lord. Had Jesus not prayed, the issue of his mission would have been different. Prayer was as real as that for him, and as important, too. For this reason, as we look further at some of these prayer situations we shall not take them for granted with an easy-going assumption of their significance. Instead we shall attempt to discover afresh their meaning for Jesus.

Beliefs That Lead to Prayer[7]

GOD'S POWER

It was pointed out earlier in this chapter that there was a direct relationship between Jesus' prayer life and his faith in the heavenly Father as he, the Son, knew him. He believed certain things about God and, therefore, he prayed in a particular way. Some

[7] The beliefs which will be considered in this section are particularly stressed in the Gospel of Luke. They are not missing from the others but the Third Evangelist majors in them.

years ago, I sought to express this truth, in reverse, in a poem. It stressed the fact that, if our faith is small, our lives will be small also:

> I have a little God,
> And hence my life is small.
> There is a limit to my prayer,
> My courage and my call,
> Distinctions come to nought
> Between the right and wrong,
> While visions hover close to earth
> And wings disdain my song.
> My nights are overcast
> And through the days I plod.
> My heart is faint,
> My hope is gone;
> I have a little God.[8]

How different it was for Jesus! He who said ". . . with God all things are possible," found ample incentive to pray in the greatness of his vision and belief. For this reason he could counsel with quiet confidence, "And I tell you, Ask, and it will be given you; seek, and you will find; knock, and it will be opened to you. For everyone who asks receives, and he who seeks finds, and to him who knocks it will be opened" (Luke 11:9-10).

GOD'S LOVE

God's power, however, is not the only basis for praying. More important is his love. And Jesus

[8] Printed in the author's *A Primer of Prayer* (Nashville: Tidings, 1949), p. 13-14.

relates this love specifically to prayer by comparing a human parent—with his limited capacity to love and his response to his child's request—to God, with his unlimited love and his eagerness to make ready answer to his children's faithful petitions. "What father among you," he inquires, "if his son asks for a fish, will instead of a fish give him a serpent; or if he asks for an egg, will give him a scorpion? If you then, who are evil, know how to give good gifts to your children, how much more will the heavenly Father give the Holy Spirit to those who ask him?" (Luke 11:11-13).[9] If we accept this interpretation of God's attitude toward man, gone is the striving. Peace takes over.

PERSISTENCE IN PRAYER

God's power and love should not only inspire us to pray with great faith; they should also encourage us to pray *with persistence.* Of all the gospel writers Luke alone gives us the teaching of Jesus on this point. It may be implied in the others, but it is not explicitly stated as the Third Evangelist records it in the twin prayer parables of Jesus, *e.g.* the parable of the Unjust Judge (18:1-8), and the parable of the Friend at Midnight (11:5-8). I wish that there were space here to dwell upon the dramatic nature of these two parables, including the unique characterizations they contain. Neither the judge, who did

[9] Matthew (7:11) carries the words "good things" in place of the Holy Spirit. The intent in both instances, however, is the same.

not fear God nor regard man, nor the parent who would not heed the request of the suppliant at his door because he was his friend, was likely to respond. But they did. Why? Just to be rid of those who were pestering them with requests.

"Is God like these two persons?" you ask. And the answer is that he is definitely not like them; in fact, he is just the opposite. The parables make their case by contrast instead of by comparison. If such self-centered individuals as these will respond for selfish reasons, *how much more* will God make willing reply to the persistent prayers of his children whom he loves.[10] We should not conclude that commendation of persistency here suggests that, if we wheedle and whine long enough, we can break down God's resistance and get what we want from an unwilling Deity. Instead, the parables encourage us to stay on the beam in prayer. It may be that by doing so we shall mature sufficiently to handle the answer when we receive it. And, in addition, there is always the chance that we shall discover a deeper need and outgrow our original petition.

The Need for Humility

The Christian's prayer begins with the basic assumption that in every situation God knows best. We could not worship or serve a divine Being of

[10] Luke introduces the parable of the Unjust Judge by saying that Jesus told it in order to teach that men ought always to pray and not lose heart (18:1).

whom this was not true. Major Whittle said of his friend, the famous evangelist Dwight L. Moody, that in prayer he was humble as a child before God, but that as he went about his work in the presence of men he was bold as a lion. The same humility was found in Brother Lawrence who wrote: "I engaged in a religious life only for the love of God, and I have endeavored to act only for Him; whatever becomes of me, whether I be lost or saved, I will always continue to act purely for the love of God. I shall have this good at least, that till death I shall have done all that is in me to love Him." [11] Humility such as this is a fragrant flower in God's garden.

How unlike this was the attitude of the Pharisee in the parable of the Pharisee and the Publican, which Luke alone of the gospel writers recorded for us (18:9-14). Of this man Jesus said that *he prayed with himself.* There was no sense of God in his life as he preened his feathers in public, and rejoiced in his own integrity. In contrast, the publican "would not even lift his eyes to heaven, but beat his breast saying, 'God, be merciful to me a sinner!'" (18:13). Such humility in prayer assured a ready hearing for him in the courts of heaven. He went down to his house justified, said our Lord.

Humility in prayer makes us gentle, willing to receive God's answer. It enables us to pray with

[11] Quoted from *The Practice of the Presence of God,* by Brother Lawrence, in *Five Spiritual Classics* (Cincinnati: Woman's Division of Christian Service, Board of Missions of The Methodist Church, 1955), p. 92.

Jesus, "Thy will be done." By it we are delivered from the sin of idolatry, which is the worship of self in the adulation of our own ego. When we are humble before God we are made pliable to receive his greatest gift—his own Presence in our lives.

The Lord's Prayer

It was in response to a request from the disciples that Jesus gave the Lord's Prayer. Luke records that it was while Jesus himself was praying that they asked him to teach them to do so. The result should be called the prayer perfect, because it is Jesus' own prayer. We have two versions of it, a shorter one in Luke (11:1-4) and a longer in Matthew (6: 9-13).[12] When this occurs, usually it is concluded that the shorter version is the original, and that the longer is a later revision. With the passing of time interpretative additions are assumed to have been added to the briefer earlier form. On this basis Luke's recital of the prayer may represent the first wording of it by Jesus himself. On the other hand, no less a distinguished New Testament scholar than E. F. Scott has argued that in this instance possibly Matthew's version is the earlier.[13] He suggests that

[12] The King James Version of Luke carries a longer form of the prayer which seems to have been adjusted to Matthew's. The Revised Standard Version of Luke follows the short text of *Codex Vaticanus* and its related documents, which gives it better manuscript support.

the Third Evangelist may have attempted to delete from the prayer any Jewish accents which it might carry, and that this shortened it.

The issue remains unsettled. A printing of Luke's form of the Lord's Prayer, as over against the familiar one that we customarily use, will immediately bring its brevity home to us.

> "Father, hallowed be thy name.
> Thy kingdom come.
> Give us each day our daily bread;
> and forgive us our sins, for we
> ourselves forgive every one who
> is indebted to us; and lead
> us not into temptation."
>
> Luke 11:2-4

It can be seen at once that this lacks the liturgical smoothness of the lengthier statement. Missing from it also are the important *"Our—who art in heaven—Thy will be done on earth as it is in heaven—But deliver us from evil."* Another difference is the use of the word "sins" (*hamartias*) in Luke, while "debts" (*opheilēmata*) is employed in Matthew. Luke's follow-through statement, however, carries the word "indebtedness" (*opheilonti*) which brings it into line with Matthew. Because of this, Matthew's "debts" was probably the original. Jews frequently referred to sins as debts, so that there is actually not as much difference between Matthew and Luke in

[13] E. F. Scott, *The Lord's Prayer* (New York: Chas. Scribner's Sons, 1951), pp. 27-30. The opening chapter, "Jesus' Conception of Prayer," is worthy of a serious reading in connection with our study.

67

regard to this petition as might at first seem to be the case.

It is the meaning of the Lord's Prayer, however, rather than these technical matters which concerns us most. Here is, in my judgment, the greatest single utterance to come from the lips of Jesus. When its phrases are interpreted in the light of his total teaching, attitudes, and ministry, the true dimensions of the prayer begin to emerge. Frequent repetitions of its words, without thoughtful consideration of their meaning, however, may dull our sensibilities, so that it will not move us greatly.

I should like to place here what I originally wrote for another study book of the Woman's Division of Christian Service concerning the Lord's Prayer and its interpretation. It is based on the longer version in Matthew, rather than upon the briefer form in Luke. But since the additional statements may well be interpretations of the Lukan form, they belong in this consideration.[14]

"The Lord's Prayer might well be called a perfect prayer. It begins as all prayers should, with a mighty sense of the greatness of God:

Our Father who art in heaven.
"God is exalted above the earth, yet not removed from the earth. He is Father of all, and men are to pray with their brothers' needs in mind, as well as their own.

[14] For instance, in Matthew *"Thy will be done on earth as it is in heaven"* carries the same meaning as the petition which immediately precedes it, which petition Luke also has, namely *"Thy kingdom come."*

Hallowed be thy name.

"Not only is God great above all others; he is also holy and righteous, and his children should revere his name, not in words alone but also in attitude and deed.

Thy kingdom come.

"Life and history are not without purpose. God's Kingdom is in the making here on earth, a great and glorious society, a brotherhood of good will.

Thy will be done
On earth as it is in heaven.

"The Kingdom of God will be a perfect expression of the perfect will of God in every human relationship.

Give us this day our daily bread.

"Material needs in the Kingdom are not beneath God's concern. Bread, books, hospitals, clothing, proper housing—all these, and more besides, are required if men are to fulfill their destiny.

And forgive us our debts,
As we also have forgiven our debtors.

"Man is more than a body; he is also a living soul. His nature is moral and spiritual basically; therefore, he needs forgiveness and must himself be forgiving. Only thus can he have fellowship with a righteous God and also with his erring brother.

And lead us not into temptation,
But deliver us from evil.

"The possibilities of evil are on every hand. Man's weakness and lack of foresight may find him unprepared to meet a sudden turn of events that tempt his soul. He needs God's help at this point.

*For thine is the kingdom and the power and
    the glory.*
"The Kingdom is God's, the power is God's, the
glory is God's. Men, however, may share in them
as children participate in their father's life. Here
is our hope and assurance of final victory." [15]

We can be certain that one prayer, the Lord's
Prayer, is in harmony with the will of God. It may
be prayed under all circumstances of life; sorrow—
sickness—death—deprivation and want—temptation
—conviction of sin, as well as on occasions of birth—
thankfulness—victory, and joy. And when we really
pray it at such times, its several petitions will light
up with special meaning, and we shall discover significance in them that had previously been hidden
from our hearts, not to mention our minds. It is both
ageless and eternal.

When Jesus Prayed

We have previously listed in this chapter the situations in which Luke notes that Jesus prayed, and
indicated something of their nature.[16] Some of them,
such as the Baptism, have already been treated with
a measure of detail and others, such as the prayers
associated with the last days in Jerusalem and the
cross, will be noted when the events inspiring them
come under immediate consideration. At this point,

[15] See the author's *Great Prayers of the Bible* (Cincinnati:
Woman's Division of Christian Service, Board of Missions of The
Methodist Church, 1947), pp. 85-86.
[16] See pp. 60-61.

however, we shall examine two occasions when Jesus withdrew for a special period of prayer. These might be called prayer retreats. They occurred when he prayed all night before selecting the twelve apostles, and when, on the Mount, he was transfigured before Peter, James, and John. In both cases we shall find that Luke emphasizes prayer in a unique way, differing from that of the other Gospels which record the same experiences.

CALLING THE TWELVE

There came a day in the developing ministry of Jesus when he chose twelve special followers. Luke 6:13 says that these were named apostles, and that they were selected from the group known as disciples. We use the two words interchangeably in popular parlance now, but actually there is a difference between them. A *disciple* refers to a follower or a learner, while an *apostle* is one who is sent, presumably to perform a specific task. Whether Jesus followed this distinction of meaning when referring to the Twelve would be difficult to determine. It may have been only Luke's particular concern to stress it, although it is interesting to note that Matthew 10:2 also refers to the Twelve in this case as apostles. Mark does not do so (3:14).

In naming the members of the group who were chosen, Luke does not refer to Thaddaeus, found in Matthew and Mark, but he does list a Judas, son of James, and they do not. These might be the same individual. The Gospel of John (14:22) also mentions a "Judas, not Iscariot" who may be the Judas, son of James, mentioned in the Gospel of Luke.

Why did our Lord make the selection we are considering? We know that it was customary in that day for a teacher to have a special company of followers. Was this the reason, or was it because of his need for companionship in the face of the growing enmity of the religious leaders toward him? In this connection it is worth noting that Luke places the calling of the Twelve immediately following his report of the rupture between Jesus and the Pharisees (6:1-11). Perhaps he was suggesting that Jesus was setting up the nucleus of a new order to take the place of the old that had rejected him.

Be this as it may, at this point we are particularly interested in the fact that Luke states that before he chose the apostles, Jesus "went out into the hills to pray; and all night he continued in prayer to God" (6:12). On the morrow he made the selection. Matthew and Mark make no mention of Jesus' praying on this occasion; Luke's stressing it is more significant, however, than their omission of it. He had been captured by the portrait of his Lord at prayer, and emphasized this aspect of his life on many occasions.

Prayer profoundly affected Jesus' choice of the Twelve. The all-night vigil made a difference in the final selection, for these were decisions of deepest consequence. What he said to God in the stillness of the dark which hung over the mountain where he was praying, we shall never know. The outcome, however, is history. The Twelve became the first official interpreters of the Faith, and their names, with the exception of Judas Iscariot, are revered beyond measure, even to the present hour.

THE TRANSFIGURATION

It was on the Mount of Transfiguration, probably Mount Hermon, that Jesus was glorified in the presence of the apostles, Peter, James, and John. He had taken them with him as he ascended the summit, where he might once again face the prospect of the death that awaited him at Jerusalem. Even though he had already concluded that the role of the Suffering Servant was his to fulfill,[17] he was not rushing into the final crisis of his life—where his own destiny and that of the human race were at stake—without full contemplation of what it meant. Here on the heights was silence for thinking—and also for praying.

Luke's account (9:28-36) of this retreat is quite similar to that found in Matthew (17:1-13) and Mark (9:2-13). All three report the company that was present, the Transfiguration of Jesus, the vision of Moses and Elijah, the approving voice of God the Father, and the insensitivity of the disciples to the significance of the event. But only Luke makes specific reference to the fact that Jesus had sought

[17] See the discussion of this issue in the previous chapter, pp. 50-51.

this solitude so that he might pray, and that it was while he was praying that the appearance of his countenance was altered (9:28-29). In the hour of great decision prayer had once again made the difference.

What specifically had prayer meant to Jesus on the Mount of Transfiguration? First of all it had brought him into the immediacy of the presence of the heavenly Father, so that he could think of the issue that was facing him in eternal and timeless terms. Under the aspect of eternity, he could view his life with the objectivity that was necessary if he were to follow the way of the cross. Next, prayer had helped Jesus to understand the experiences of Moses and Elijah, as these were recorded in the Scriptures. They, too, had known rejection at the hands of the nation but each had been vindicated by God. The past became alive for him and ministered to his questing spirit. Again, prayer had enabled him to say "yes" to the cross. Luke alone notes that it was about his death that Moses and Elijah had spoken to Jesus. Furthermore, as in prayer Jesus affirmed his willingness to do the Father's will, the glory of the Eternal had transfigured him, so that his entire being shone with divine radiance. And finally, prayer had opened his soul to hear the commendation of God, even as he had heard it at the Baptism.

The author of Hebrews also shows a marked understanding of the prayer life of Jesus. He says, "In the days of his flesh, Jesus offered up prayers and supplications, with loud cries and tears, to him who was able to save him from death, and he was heard for his godly fear" (Hebrews 5:7). Let us leave it here. Rather, let us take up our own prayer life now, touched by the praying of Jesus himself, as Luke recreates it vividly before us.

Christ and the Kingdom ═══════

MARK INDICATES THAT JESUS opened his mission with this announcement: "The time is fulfilled, and the kingdom of God is at hand" (Mark 1:15). Although Luke does not carry this particular statement in his writing, he does make it clear that the Kingdom was a constant concern of Jesus throughout his ministry. For instance, he notes on one occasion that our Lord ". . . spoke to them of the kingdom of God, and cured those who had need of healing" (Luke 9:11). And on another, Luke relates that when Jesus sent out the seventy on an evangelistic tour, he told them to speak to the people in the villages this word: "The kingdom of God has come near to you" (Luke 10:9).

The Nature of the Kingdom

What is this Kingdom to which Jesus refers? Those who first heard him herald it were not uninformed about it. Interpreted as God's righteous rule among men, it had been proclaimed as the goal of history for generations before Jesus. This was a many-sided dream, and included such features as material plenty, peace, the judgment of evil men and nations, and a beatific blessing for the faithful. Usually its realization was associated with the coming of the Messiah who would reign on earth as God's anointed (Isaiah 9:6-7; 11:1-10). To expect that Jehovah God would express himself among men through the person of a deliverer seemed quite within reason. Why should he not bring the world he had created under his sway, at long last? The reign of God among men was the logical outcome of the character and power of the Almighty, which had been made known to the nation Israel in the covenant and commandments, as well as through the preaching of the prophets.

We have already seen that Jesus received a call to be the Messiah at his baptism, and that in the wilderness of temptation he struggled to decide what type of messiah God wanted him to be. He rejected the idea of becoming an economic liberator, of using temporary spectacular methods, and of establishing an earthly rule such as Rome's. Instead, he would become a prophetic servant who would spend his life in helping the needy and neglected, and in proclaiming the day of God's gracious visitation. Now the point is this. *If Jesus were to be this kind of messiah, the Kingdom must be this kind of Kingdom.* The two were inseparable.

It is in the Lord's Prayer that we find the most definitive statement concerning the nature of the Kingdom, that is, in the longer version of the prayer which Matthew carries (6:9-13). Here we read,

> "Thy kingdom come,
> Thy will be done,
> On earth as it is in heaven."
> Matthew 6:10

The second sentence here, as generally in Hebrew poetry, repeats the sentiment of the first sentence. The Kingdom, therefore, is to be the full expression of God's will on earth even as it is perfectly realized in heaven. This rules out certain features in the traditional expectation of the Jews; the Kingdom is to be religious and ethical, rather than economic, political, and military. Between God and man, and between man and man, God's will shall prevail. This is the kingdom of God, nothing less.

We have but to ask what changes in life today would take place if God's will were to be fully expressed in such a fashion, to realize the monumental incisiveness of this petition. Insert it in any given situation and the results would be quite startling, if not actually staggering. International relations, national and local government, community life, management and labor disputes, interracial fellowship, the home, and individual living—all these are areas in which the heavenly Father has a will, a good will, and a loving will. To search for it and to attempt by God's grace to fulfill it remains life's greatest adventure for the Christian. In the final analysis, this is a very personal call—to recognize and follow God's will. As T. W. Manson has reminded us, the petition means "Thy will be done, *and done by me.*"

Healing and the Kingdom

We have noted that the Kingdom is the reign of God on earth, interpreted as the expression of his will in every personal and social relationship. This might be called a definition *in principle,* open-ended to the extent that the details need to be filled in by every person and every generation. In addition to this, however, Jesus said and did a number of specific things that indicate something of the character of God's will.

For instance, when our Lord sent forth the Twelve on an evangelistic mission, Luke says that he "gave them power and authority over all demons and to cure diseases, and he sent them out to preach the kingdom of God and to heal" (9:1-2). Likewise when he sent out the seventy on a similar mission, they were told to "heal the sick" and to say to men, "The kingdom of God has come near to you" (10: 9). In both instances healing the sick was a means of fulfilling the will of God. In addition, Luke records that Jesus said on one occasion ". . . if it is by the finger of God that I cast out demons, then the kingdom of God has come upon you" (11:20).

The four Gospels record some twenty-five instances of Jesus' healing the sick.[1] Of this number, five are noted by Luke alone,[2] while Matthew carries two that are found only in his Gospel.[3] John reports four such cases.[4] This may not seem to be a large number, but there are other general references to healing such as that which is given at the close of the first day's ministry at Capernaum.[5] All in all, Jesus' healing ministry was probably extensive.

The types of disorders which Jesus healed were varied.[6] They included demon-possession, curvature of the spine, epilepsy, leprosy, paralysis, blindness, dropsy, fever, deafness and dumbness, bleeding, a maimed hand, and a severed bodily member, and death. Some understanding is needed concerning our Lord's purpose in this ministry. It was not to prove that he was the Messiah or a divine Being, as is sometimes urged, that he performed these deeds of mercy. Rather, they were an expression of God's visitation in the Kingdom. They belonged to his vocation as the Messiah.

In connection with the healing ministry of Jesus as it relates to the Kingdom, particular attention should be given to the casting out of demons. It was

[1] The number cannot be exact because of possible overlapping. For instance, is the healing of the official's son (John 4:46-54) the same event as the healing of the centurion's slave (Luke 7:1-10)?

[2] Luke 7:11-17; 13:11-17; 14:1-6; 17:11-19; 22:50-51.

[3] Matthew 9:27-31; 9:32-33.

[4] John 4:46-54; 5:1-9; 9:1-7; 11:38-44.

[5] "Now when the sun was setting, all those who had any that were sick with various diseases brought them to him; and he laid his hands on every one of them and healed them" (Luke 4:40).

[6] For a rather full treatment of the healing ministry of Jesus, see the author's *The Life and Teachings of Jesus* (Nashville: Abingdon Press, 1955), Chapter 12.

accepted among the Jews in that day that the world was temporarily under the control of Beelzebul, the prince of demons, and his host of evil spirits who did his bidding (Luke 11:15).[7] The thralldom of this belief was unbearable. Sickness and all manner of misfortunes were attributed to these forces, particularly when they indwelt a human person. Whenever Jesus was brought face to face with illness, therefore, what it really amounted to was that he saw himself in a direct conflict with Beelzebul. And his ability to cast out demons was an expression of his greater power. Through the kingdom of God the kingdom of evil was being routed. So, in addition to being a deed of mercy and love, every act of healing represented a victory over the forces of the evil spirit. Thus their strangle hold upon men was being broken.[8]

In his healing activity Jesus must not be regarded as a kind of magician whose touch was magical. These deeds of mercy were moral and spiritual; in most cases they required faith, either the person's own or that of another (Luke 8:48; 5:20). They also took from Jesus some personal strength so that he felt power go forth from his being. On the occasion of the healing of the woman who had the issue of blood, he said as much (Luke 8:46).

For several centuries after the death of Jesus the

[7] The King James Version was Beelzebub. The Greek is Beelzebul. Another name for him is Satan.

[8] Some of the particular instances of casting out of demons in Luke are: The healing in the synagogue (4:31-37), the case of the Gerasene demoniac (8:26 ff.), the curing of the epileptic boy (9:37 f.), and the overcoming of the dumb spirit (11:14).

Church continued the work of healing as a regular part of its ministry. Then it was allowed to lapse, although probably at no time has there been none of it practiced among Christians. Today there is a renaissance of interest in this service. Psychosomatic medicine (which applies the principles of psychology in the treatment of physical disease and thereby approaches some of the aspects of spiritual healing) has seemingly given it some scientific standing. In the face of the facts, however, it is difficult to see why Christian healing ever needed endorsement, even though extremists have sometimes made it appear in a bad light. Quite recently the Protestant Episcopal Church has officially approved several litanies of healing for use in its communion. If spiritual healing is practiced in accordance with Jesus' own understanding of its meaning and place in the kingdom of God, we have nothing but good to expect from it.

Our Lord regarded health of body and mind as characteristic of life in the Kingdom. Healing was, therefore, an outreach of the love of God. It was to be sought within the will of the heavenly Father, as were all other expressions of the Kingdom. Prayer for physical renewal is therefore not only proper; it is also a spiritual obligation.

Forgiveness and the Kingdom

Just as man does not live by bread alone, he also does not live by health of body alone. His nature is moral and spiritual as well as physical. The Kingdom, therefore, includes forgiveness as well as healing. This truth was brought out in the account of the curing of the paralytic who was let down into Jesus' presence through an opening in the roof of a home (Luke 5:17-26). Even though his four friends had brought the man to Jesus for healing, our Lord said, first of all, to him, "Man, your sins are forgiven you."

Much speculation has occurred as to why this paralytic was forgiven before he was healed. It has been suggested that sin had caused his illness. Did not the teaching of the rabbis say that no man rises from his sick-pallet until he has first been forgiven? And, from our own standpoint, have we not learned that a sick conscience sometimes expresses itself in a sick body? [9] It is, therefore, quite possible that the man's sin had been responsible for his paralysis. On the other hand, it must not be forgotten that Jesus did not believe that misfortune was *invariably* due to sin. For instance, he distinctly said that the eighteen upon whom the tower of Siloam had fallen and the Galileans whom Pilate had killed were not any more sinful than were their brothers (Luke 13:1-5). But he also warned that the death that comes through sin is just as deadly.

Our main reason for referring to the account of the healing of the paralytic, however, is that it shows Jesus as declaring that the man's sins were forgiven. This was a part of his kingdom ministry. We can also see this in the narrative of the sinful woman who

[9] See Psalm 32 for an amazingly frank statement of this truth.

interrupted a dinner in the home of a Pharisee in order to seek out Jesus (Luke 7:36-50).[10] Her repentance expressed itself in the loving act of washing his feet with her tears, and wiping them with her hair. Our Lord said to Simon the host, ". . . her sins, which are many, are forgiven, for she loved much;" And to the woman, he added, "Your faith has saved you; go in peace."

A discussion of forgiveness as an aspect of life in the Kingdom would not be complete without a reference to Jesus' word to one of the two thieves who were crucified with him (Luke 23:39-43). Something in the lordly manner in which Christ bore his suffering impressed this distraught man in his dark hour. Seemingly, it called to the surface the basic goodness that was in his soul, in spite of what he had done and become. So he said, "Jesus, remember me when you come in your kingly power," and our Lord replied, "Truly, I say to you, today you will be with me in Paradise." The usual interpretation that is given to these words is that Jesus was declaring that the man's sins had been forgiven. It should be noted that Luke alone of all the gospel writers has preserved this important word from the cross.

A point of difference among biblical interpreters is whether or not Jesus himself was forgiving the sins of these and other persons, or whether he was announcing the forgiveness of the heavenly Father.

[10] This appears to be another version of the story in Mark 14:3-9 and Matthew 26:6-13. Here the setting is the home of Simon the leper at Bethany, while Luke's account concerns Simon the Pharisee. Compare it also with the account of how Mary of Bethany washed Jesus feet in John 12:1-8.

Surely God alone can forgive sins. And if Jesus himself were forgiving the sinful, it could only mean that in his life the forgiving love of God was present. This much is certain: Men have been confessing their sins to Christ ever since the days of his flesh, and in doing so, have come to know the forgiveness of God himself. This is a matter of record rather than of speculation.

The new life with healing and forgiveness which attended the ministry of Jesus, and which was characteristic of the kingdom of God, is reminiscent of Isaiah's words to the discouraged exiles in Babylon. In fact we have a reflection of Isaiah in the reply Jesus gave to the disciples of John the Baptist, who had come to inquire whether he were the Christ. He said to them: "Go and tell John what you have seen and heard: the blind receive their sight, the lame walk, lepers are cleansed, and the deaf hear, the dead are raised up, the poor have good news preached to them" (Luke 7:22). How like the words of the ancient prophet!

> Then the eyes of the blind shall be opened,
>   and the ears of the deaf unstopped;
> then shall the lame man leap like a hart,
>   and the tongue of the dumb sing for joy.
> For waters shall break forth in the wilderness,
>   and streams in the desert;
> the burning sand shall become a pool,
>   and the thirsty ground springs of water;
>   Isaiah 35:5-7

Citizens of the Kingdom

But what marked a citizen of the kingdom of God?
How did he live? Just as in Matthew's report of the
Sermon on the Mount (chapters 5-7), so in what has
been called in Luke the Sermon on the Plain or
Level Place (6:17-49), we are given a selection of
the teachings of Jesus which may be regarded as
indicating the marks of citizenship in the Kingdom.
In both cases we probably have a collection of
teachings which Jesus uttered at different times, although the tradition of a particular sermon which
remained vivid in the memory of his followers may
also have been drawn upon.[11]

Luke gives us the familiar beatitudes (6:20-22)
as a part of the sermon, just as Matthew does. And,
as in the case of his version of the Lord's Prayer,
the form differs somewhat. In the Third Gospel they
are briefer, fewer in number, and are followed by
a series of Woes (Luke 6:24-26) which are the direct opposite of the blessings. Too much may be made
of these differences by biblical interpreters. For instance, in Jesus' total message, the "poor" (Luke
6:20) and the "poor in spirit" (Matthew 5:3) are
not two different groups of persons. What we probably have here is an interpretative elaboration by
Matthew of an earlier and briefer version, in which
the original beatitudes are spiritualized. In both
cases the blessings of God in the Kingdom belong to

[11] A number of Matthew's quoted words of Jesus in the Sermon
on the Mount are found in different settings in the other Gospels.
Because Luke was writing to Gentile readers primarily, he
omitted the sayings in Matthew (5-7) which deal with the Law.

the pious poor, the neglected hungry, the broken hearted, and the persecuted. And what is remarkable in all of this is that usually these unwelcome states of poverty, hunger, heartbreak, and persecution, turn out to be emblems of potential citizenship in the Kingdom. It is for those who endure these afflictions that God's special favor is intended. What a reversal!

There is a reversal also in the attitude of the kingdom citizen toward others. He loves his enemies in the sense that he returns good for evil, and expresses good will toward them (Luke 6:27-36). In this he is like the heavenly Father, who makes his sun to rise on the evil and the good, and who sends his rain on the just and unjust. In addition, faultfinding is ruled out in those who belong to the kingdom of God (Luke 6:37-42). They are delivered from being caustically critical because they examine their own lives before criticizing others. This makes them humble and generous. All they do is done out of a sincere and good heart. It is not "put on" from the outside, and their deeds, therefore, indicate their devotion (Luke 6:43-45).

The Sermon on the Plain in Luke (6:17-49), like the Sermon on the Mount in Matthew (5:1—7:27), closes with the parable of the Two Foundations (Luke 6:46-49). This remarkable passage stresses the relationship between hearing and doing, and is intended to be a warning to those who take the gospel of the Kingdom lightly. Life's storms will find them unprepared to withstand the strain, and their ruin will be great.

When Is the Kingdom?

But when is the Kingdom coming? We today speak of working for its advent, and picture such gains as the reduction of poverty and the overcoming of evil as an evidence of its progress. We do not, however, consider that it has fully come as long as war continues and greed enslaves so many. This is our view. Was it the view of Jesus?

The answer to this question is that Jesus believed that the Kingdom was both present and future. Even though evil had not yet been fully routed, whenever men took the kingdom attitude toward God and their fellows, the Kingdom itself was there. On one occasion Jesus said ". . . behold, the kingdom of God is *in the midst of you*" (Luke 17:21).[12] At yet another time he said, "The law and the prophets were until John; since then the good news of the kingdom of God is preached, and *every one enters it violently*" (Luke 16:16).[13] We have already noted that our Lord considered his casting out of demons an indication of the actual presence of the Kingdom (Luke 11:20).[14] These statements and the total tone of his preaching make it quite clear that he regarded the Kingdom as having already come. If men would but look around them, and take note of the wonderful things that were happening wherever he went, they

[12] Italics are the author's. In the King James Version this verse is translated "the kingdom of God is within you." This is not at variance with the Revised Standard Version because, if it is within us, it is also present.

[13] Italics are the author's.

[14] See page 80.

would see for themselves that the kingdom was come.

On the other hand, there are statements of our Lord that indicate that he sometimes thought of the Kingdom as a future event. Luke carries verses which support this view, as well as those already cited which confirm the belief that the Kingdom had already come in their midst. When Jesus was at table with his disciples, in the Upper Room, he turned to them on that final night of his life, and said "I tell you that from now on I shall not drink of the fruit of the vine *until the kingdom of God comes*" (Luke 22: 18).[15] Even though the King would be killed on the morrow, the Kingdom would still come! This points to the future.

There is only an apparent contradiction in Jesus' teaching that the kingdom of God was both present and future. Whenever men lived as citizens of the Kingdom, at least in that particular situation, it was really present. But it would not be fully come in its glorious expanse until it was universally present.

How Comes the Kingdom?

In answering the question as to how the Kingdom comes we again meet with what appear to be opposing viewpoints in Jesus' own words. On occasion it seems that he thought of men as contributing to its coming, and yet again, that it was God alone who could bring it to pass. On the one hand, he told his

[15] Italics are the author's.

followers to "seek his kingdom" (Luke 12:31); they should "strive to enter by the narrow door" (Luke 13:24), and count the cost, lest they become disillusioned and fall away. Then they would be like salt that has lost its savor (Luke 14:25-35).

On the other hand, Jesus referred to the Kingdom as God's gift. Once he said "Fear not, little flock, for it is your Father's good pleasure to give you the kingdom" (Luke 12:32). Thus, we have but to receive it. This, however, we should do "as a little child" if we are to enter (Luke 18:17), humbly, expectantly, and joyfully. Here again, the truth is so all-encompassing that it can only be expressed in a paradox. God's giving and our striving go together. As God gives, we seek, and as we seek, we discover that God gives. No person can claim that he brought the Kingdom into being by his own efforts; yet without men—God's children—there would be no Kingdom.

There are other seemingly contradictory statements in Jesus' teaching concerning the "how" of the coming of the Kingdom. He said that it was like leaven that causes the meal to rise (Luke 13:20-21), and also like a grain of mustard seed which grew to become a tree that gave sanctuary to the birds (Luke 13:18-19). These parables suggest a gradual process of growth. As such they were stressed by those who were energetic in the social gospel movement. The idea of *progress* fitted so perfectly into this conception.

But there were further sayings of our Lord that referred to the coming of the Kingdom in apocalyptic terms, that is, they spoke of its coming suddenly, down from above, from outside and beyond man's sphere. It was to come from heaven as a sudden interjection into our world—judging it, overthrowing it, and replacing it with God's righteous rule (Luke 21:5-36). The picture that is given includes famine, earthquakes, war, and cosmic distresses, before the final consummation of history when the Son of man comes "in a cloud with power and great glory" (Luke 21:27) to rule in his kingdom. Albert Schweitzer made this view central in his interpretation of Jesus' teaching.[16] This kind of thinking was prevalent in our Lord's day and the conclusion is sometimes drawn that Jesus embraced it fully and that he was an apocalyptist, wholly and completely.

Here again, it seems to me that we must keep both points of view in mind at one and the same time, the gradual coming and the apocalyptic coming of the Kingdom. There were occasions when Jesus spoke in terms applicable to the apocalyptic view and times when he spoke of the establishment of the Kingdom on earth through the preaching of his followers. To emphasize either approach to the exclusion of the other is unhistorical, because both are present in Jesus' teaching. And experience will bear out the truth in each.

In all of this it must not be forgotten that Jesus was sometimes quite poetical and metaphorical in his expressions, teaching through parable and symbol. We are apt to err if we interpret his phrases

[16] Albert Schweitzer: *Quest of the Historical Jesus* (New York: The Macmillan Co., 1948).

too literally. What he wanted most to say, in my judgment, was that *God has a gracious gift for man; it is the Kingdom. As we seek it, God will give it. If we neglect it, judgment will follow. It is present already where Christ is served, yet it has not fully come. In the end, however, the total Kingdom as the goal of history will be realized; God's will shall be done on earth even as it is in heaven. He will see to it himself. Meanwhile, we shall strive, pray, work, and live as its citizens.*

VII

The Gospel of Love ═══

THE GREAT COMMANDMENT—"Thou shalt love"—is found in all three Gospels. In this summons Jesus called upon his followers to love God completely and manfully. Matthew (22:37-39) and Mark (12:29-31) indicate that it is Jesus who states it, while Luke (10:25-28) notes that it is a lawyer, and Jesus gives hearty approval to the expression. The lawyer had asked Jesus what he should do to inherit eternal life. He replied "What is written in the law? How do you read?" Then the lawyer answered, "You shall love the Lord your God with all your heart, and with all your soul, and with all your strength, and with all your mind; and your neighbor as yourself."

These words can be seen to contain the Shema of Deuteronomy (6:5), which was the keystone of the Jewish faith. The distinguished Hebrew scholar,

C. G. Montefiore, has commented that Jesus shows himself to be a true Jew in the statement of the Great Commandment. But our Lord moved beyond the Shema to include a further injunction. Man must love his neighbor as himself. This is found in Leviticus 19:18. The uniqueness of Jesus here lies in the fact that he combined the two: love of man for God and love of man for man. It is like the cross in which the upright unites heaven and earth, and the crossbar binds together all mankind.

Luke also joins with Matthew in presenting another word of Jesus which suggests the second part of the Great Commandment. We refer to it as the *Golden Rule*. In both cases it appears in the Sermon on the Mount (*Plain* or *Level Place* in Luke) in connection with our Lord's teaching concerning man's relation to other persons. This, again, is a part of his emphasis upon love: "And as you wish that men would do to you, do so to them" (Luke 6:31). Just before stating these words, Jesus had been talking about loving one's enemies and turning the other cheek, so that they may be regarded as a kind of summary of this instruction. Goodwill is to be shown to all, even as we would wish that goodwill should be shown to us.

There is a special turn of thought in the Golden Rule which should not be missed. It does not say that we should do to others what we think should be done for them from where we stand. Instead, it implies that we should treat them as we would wish to be treated *if we were in their situation*. This requires that we identify ourselves with others in sincere concern, making their interests and needs our responsibility. Actually, the principle of the cross itself is involved in the attitude of love which the teaching enjoins. The Golden Rule demands true respect for personality in that it does not override the way other people think, their longings, and their basic motives.

The Golden Rule has led kings to live as commoners in order that they might learn the true feelings of their people. It has sent seminary students into factories to work side by side with laborers, so that they might establish a bond of understanding with them and better serve as pastors in the future. The Christian call to love is not a summons to patronize others by showering them with sentimentality, but an invitation to thoughtful identification in which we love them as we love ourselves.

CHRIST'S LOVE FOR PEOPLE

In order to do this it is necessary to meet people personally. Long-distance contacts will not do. Jesus is our example here. He was not an ascetic who withdrew from society. Instead, he mingled with the folks of his day in close personal fellowship throughout his ministry. Crowds seemed to stimulate him, but he was never more effective than in small groups or in individual interviews. For this reason his thinking was personalized and not abstract.

On one occasion Luke says that the "people pressed upon him to hear the word of God" (Luke

5:1); on another he says that "the crowd welcomed him" (Luke 8:40). Yet again, we read of his moving on to another community and that "when the crowds learned it, they followed him; and he welcomed them and spoke to them of the kingdom of God" (Luke 9:11). This was the occasion on which he fed the five thousand. It was when "great multitudes accompanied him" (Luke 14:25), that he gave his teaching concerning the need to put God first, even before family and one's own life. Finally, at the time of his death, Luke says that the "multitudes . . . assembled to see the sight" (Luke 23:48). There were people everywhere and always where Jesus was concerned.

I do not know whether or not there were "society editors" in that day who spread the news of what was happening. If so, Jesus' name must have been mentioned frequently, for the Gospels often indicate that he was invited out to dine. And the interesting thing about it is that his hosts included Pharisees, outcasts such as tax collectors, and personal friends. His enemies used these social occasions against him, even calling him a glutton and a drunkard (Luke 7:34). But he regarded them as an opportunity to draw near to those who needed him. Once when the company included those whom the respectables considered sinners, Jesus replied to their criticism that he ate with the riffraff by saying, "Those who are well have no need of a physician, but those who are sick; I have not come to call the righteous, but sinners to repentance" (Luke 5:31).

In loving others as one loves oneself the enmity of fellowmen who would do us harm presents a special problem. Man's natural inclination to retaliate by returning evil for evil makes love difficult. When we feel particularly pious we may talk sentimentally about the beauty of loving our enemies; but faced with evil acts and intentions, we find it difficult to "do good to those who hate us."

We usually think of Jesus' teaching concerning love for our enemies as applying chiefly to our national foes in times of war. The self-sacrifice of pacifists bears telling testimony to the Christian witness at such times.[1] And even among those who feel that it is necessary, practically speaking, to bear arms, there are many who do so at the cost of deep and disturbing qualms of conscience. Make no mistake about it, the words, "But I say to you that hear, Love your enemies, do good to those who hate you, bless those who curse you, pray for those who abuse you. To him who strikes you on the cheek, offer the other also" (Luke 6:27-29); these words have gotten under the skins of his followers through the centuries.

But it is not only in the dramatic issues of war and peace that this injunction of our Lord applies. The situations of everyday living which involve human ambition, greed, and the clash of personalities also confront us with the constant need to be loving, to

[1] See G. H. C. Macgregor, *The New Testament Basis of Pacifism* (New York: Fellowship of Reconciliation, 1937).

return good for evil. The word for love which is used here is *agape*. It means a self-giving kind of love, as over against selfish sex-love (*erōs*) or friendship (*philia*). As such, it is the unique Christian kind of love. Paul employs *agape* in his hymn of love that appears in First Corinthians 13. Because our use of the word "love" is so indiscriminate, it is difficult to find an equivalent for *agape* in the English language. Perhaps the attitude of indomitable goodwill comes as near to it as anything else, since it suggests an active, outgoing relationship rather than gushing sentimentality.

The motive for loving one's enemies is to be found in the character of God himself. He does it; so should we. It is as simple and as demanding as that. This is what Jesus said: "But love your enemies, and do good, and lend, expecting nothing in return; and your reward will be great, and you will be sons of the Most High; for he is kind to the ungrateful and the selfish. Be merciful, even as your Father is merciful" (Luke 6:35-36). The Christian ethic is absolute in the sense that it holds before us, human as we are, the perfection that is in God.

Much time may be spent in arguing as to whether or not it is possible to attain this ideal. And the answer, of course, is that by ourselves it is not possible. And yet we are called upon to do so. How shall we escape from this impasse? Only in Christ can we as Christians love our enemies. It takes his example, his grace, and his power. Luke was later to record the dying prayer of Stephen, who was the first Christian martyr. As the stones were being hurled upon him, he prayed, "Lord, do not hold this sin against them" (Acts 7:60). How like the petition from the cross, found in Luke alone, "Father, forgive them, for they know not what they do" (Luke 23:34)! It seems clear to me that Stephen was able to pray for his enemies only because he held before his eyes the picture of his Lord as he prayed for his persecutors.

Love Toward Outcasts

Caste was an important concern to the Jews who first heard Jesus. It determined their social relationships and religious standing as well. Members of certain professions such as tax collecting and hide tanning were outcasts. Sinners and Gentiles were also beyond the pale. Fellowship with those who were ceremonially unclean, because they did not observe the food laws and washings, was forbidden. And lepers also were not allowed to keep company with others, until they had secured a writ of cleansing from the priests.

All of this made living difficult. These taboos were originally intended to preserve the purity and individuality of the nation's life, and as such their intention was worthy. But, as practiced, they resulted in snobbery and cruel ostracism. To be an outcast in Jewish society was to suffer. It was made quite obvious to the outcast that he did not belong among his fellows, and this rejection was cruel in the extreme.

Whether or not it was because Luke lived as a

Gentile where there were Jews, even before he became a Christian, or for some other unknown reason, the fact remains that he made the fellowship of Jesus with outcasts a major consideration in his Gospel. A number of special cases are found in his writing, pointed up so that this issue cannot be missed. There was the feast which Levi the publican gave to celebrate his becoming a disciple, and which Jesus himself attended, much to the disgust of the righteous Pharisees (5:29 ff.); the intrusion of the woman who was a sinner at the dinner party in the house of Simon the Pharisee (7:36 ff.); the parable of the Good Samaritan (10:29 ff.); the meal at which Jesus refused to participate in the ceremonial washing in order to show its insincerity (11:37 ff.); the parable of the Great Banquet where room was made for outcasts, and Gentiles (14:21 ff.); the occasion for telling the parables of the Lost Sheep, the Lost Coin, and the Lost Sons, the latter usually called the Prodigal Son (15:1 ff.); the healing of the ten lepers when only one of them, a Samaritan, returned to express his gratitude (17:17 ff.); and the conversion of the tree-climbing Zacchaeus (19:1 ff.). Of these eight mentioned, five are found in Luke alone.[2]

There is not too much difference between caste systems in Jesus' day as Luke knew them—and de-

[2] These are the parable of the Good Samaritan, the parable of the Great Banquet, the occasion for the three parables in Luke 15, the healing of the ten lepers, and the conversion of Zacchaeus. The forgiving of the sinful woman may have a counterpart in Matthew 26:6 ff., Mark 14:3 ff., and John 12:1 ff.

plored them—and those of the present. Whenever men consider others of their fellows as second class citizens, to say nothing of regarding them as second class persons, the result is the same. It does not take too much judgment or imagination to conclude that, if he were writing now, Luke would emphasize the words and deeds of Jesus which obviously apply to racial discrimination and other forms of ostracism which obtain throughout the world today.

Even among the members of a single race, we practice caste. There are wealthy churches, middle-class churches, and impoverished churches, and the members of one congregation do not feel at home with the others. Some believe that our larger denominations have become sophisticated and are neglecting the poor and needy in our communities, because, in our estimation, they "would not fit" into our beautiful cathedral-type churches. A number of the smaller denominations have moved into areas where we once served, and are building new congregations composed of those who no longer feel welcome among us.

Caste continues in our communities, in high schools, colleges, women's clubs, and luncheon groups. We may not have the same bases for discrimination today, but do we not still have those who "belong" and those who do not? People are made to feel inferior, now as they were then. Is there much difference between the Pharisees and us in this regard?

Although Luke does not give as detailed a consideration of marriage and divorce as is found in Matthew and Mark, his concern for the home and children is no less marked than theirs (Luke 18:15-17). As a Gentile he was not reared within the Hebrew tradition of family life. This may account for the fact that when referring to marriage, he does not carry Jesus' words concerning Moses and the law of divorce. Matthew, however, takes this tradition as he found it in Mark and quotes it fully, even editing it at one important point.

Marriage among the Jews in Jesus' day was under the constant threat of dissolution. This was no less true in the Greco-Roman society. Divorce was easy and often depended upon the whim of the husband rather than upon deeper causes. A wife could not divorce her husband, but the husband could separate from his wife at will, needing only to give her a bill of divorcement (Deuteronomy 24:1-4). In such a situation there was little respect for the personality of the wife, respect such as love requires. The effect of this insecurity upon married women and the children in the household must have been considerable. And had it not been for the strict moral code of the Jews, marriage among them would have been an unsubstantial affair.

It is in the light of this fact that Luke's quotation of Jesus' teaching on divorce has an unusual significance. On one occasion our Lord said "Every one who divorces his wife and marries another commits adultery, and he who marries a woman divorced from her husband commits adultery" (Luke 16:18). Matthew and Mark give the setting for these words; Luke does not. It was the Pharisees who raised the question, "Is it lawful for a man to divorce his wife?" (Mark 10:2). Mark says in addition that they made this inquiry "in order to test him." (See also Matthew 19:3.) Presumably they expected that he would be more liberal than they, and therefore subject to criticism.

A reading of Jesus' words as reported by Luke suggests that he forbade divorce completely. The Roman Catholic Church has followed this interpretation. Some Protestant groups, however, have not been as strict as this in interpreting our Lord's statement. First of all, they do not regard Jesus as a legalist, and do not think that he was legislating in this teaching. Instead, he may have been asserting an ideal in the strongest possible terms, using hyperbole to emphasize his point, as he often did.[3]

Another reason for not interpreting the statement of Jesus on divorce, as reported in Luke, as absolutely prohibiting the act, is that Matthew, in his version of the teaching carries an exception. If unchastity ("fornication" in K.J.V.) is involved in the situation, divorce is permitted. It may well be that this is an interpretation, or even, as some scholars allege, an interpolation, on Matthew's part. But this does not mean that it may not be more nearly what Jesus

[3] Compare Mark 9:43 ff., where Jesus refers to cutting off one's hand and foot, as well as to plucking out one's eye. This is an obvious exaggeration, not to be taken literally.

meant by his teaching on divorce than the stricter statement, legalistically interpreted.

On the other hand, to hold that under certain conditions Jesus permitted divorce is not to say that he took a light view of the marriage vows and favored easy separation. Not at all! Both Matthew and Mark quote him as saying that Moses gave the law for divorce "because of their hardness of heart" (Matthew 19:8; Mark 10:5). It was not in the original intention of God that a marriage should be broken. The relationship was to be for life; as our marriage vows state, "until death do us part." Therefore, unless the continuation of a marriage is demoralizing to all concerned, including the children, the ties should not be severed. Love must go all the way before divorce is sought. As I have written elsewhere, "Unless divorce is a love act in the best interests of all parties concerned, as Jesus interpreted love, it is out of line with his teachings." [4]

CHRIST'S CONCERN FOR WOMEN

There is yet another of Luke's special interests in the Third Gospel which may be appropriately considered at this point. It is the place and the opportunities of women in the kingdom of God. In an oriental society where women were given a subordinate place this is quite significant. It might be said that Luke foresaw the emancipation of women which would come with the spread of the gospel

[4] See the author's *The Life and Teachings of Jesus,* p. 207.

more fully than did any other New Testament author. As in most of the issues where he shows a marked concern, he does not deliberately utter pronouncements on the subject. Instead, he makes it a point to record incidents in the ministry of Jesus where women are involved and play a significant part.

For instance, in the course of describing one of our Lord's preaching tours he notes that "the twelve were with him, and also some women who had been healed of evil spirits and infirmities: "Mary, called Magdalene, from whom seven demons had gone out, and Joanna, the wife of Chuza, Herod's steward, and Susanna, and many others, who provided for them out of their means" (Luke 8:2-3). It is suggested here that women helped in these team responsibilities and also supported the cause financially. This reference informs us further that Mary Magdalene had been healed of a mental illness, and that some of the women who followed him were persons of position and wealth, as in the case of Joanna who was the wife of the overseer of Herod's estates.

It is easy for us to read of these things and to pass right over their significance. We are so accustomed to accepting women's contributions to the Christian cause that we miss the point. The typical rabbi would not have included women on his staff.[5] They were even required to sit in the balcony at the synagogue service, and could not enter as much of the Temple at Jerusalem as the men, a special court being assigned to them. This was a type of segrega-

[5] See C. G. Montefiore, *Rabbinic Literature and Gospel Teaching* (New York: The Macmillan Co., 1930), p. 217.

tion, no less. But one has only to compare through-out the centuries the status of women in countries where Christianity has spread with that in non-Christian countries to see what a difference Jesus has made. Some change in this respect is occurring in oriental and Moslem lands in our day, but though unrecognized as such, much of it is a spill-over from western culture which, in turn, was influenced by Jesus. He remains the chief emancipator of women in history.

Additional references to women and their place in the work of the Kingdom which Luke records,[6] include the stories of the widow of Nain whose son Jesus raised from the dead (Luke 7:11-17), the woman who was forgiven in the home of Simon the Pharisee (Luke 7:36-50), the lady who touched the hem of his garment and was healed (Luke 8:43-48), the sisters Mary and Martha who received Jesus into their home (Luke 10:38-42), and the "daughters of Jerusalem" whom Jesus comforted as they wept for him when he carried his cross to Golgotha (Luke 23:28). Women are also mentioned as performing burial services in connection with our Lord's death (Luke 23:55), and as coming to the tomb on the first day of the week to complete their task, only to discover that he had risen (Luke 24:1-11).

We have seen that to love one's neighbor as one-self has far-reaching implications in social relationships. It is the characteristic Christian teaching con-

[6] See also "The Gospel According to 31 Women" in Margaret Applegarth's *Twelve Baskets Full* (New York: Harper & Bros., 1957), and Edith Deen's *All of the Women of the Bible* (New York: Harper & Bros., 1955).

cerning our attitude toward our fellowmen, and rests on the Christian's conception of himself as a being created in the image of God, and of all men as having a like origin. We are never to forget that our worth is such that Christ lived and died for us. Otherwise we shall miss the point entirely.

VIII

The Coin of the Realm

THE LOVE OF RICHES is not confined to the twentieth century—nor was it to the fifteenth, nor the fifth. Our Lord himself had so much to say about wealth that it is clearly evident that men in the first century were also enamoured of it. It is startling to realize that the teachings of Jesus concerning money ("mammon" in Luke 16:13) are more numerous than his utterances concerning almost any other subject, including faith and love. Evidently he had observed that here was an area where persons were affected by the attitude they held in ways that determined their destiny.

Jesus' references to money, its use and misuse, were not academic. He was not proposing a theory of wealth *per se;* instead he was handling a very personal problem for most people, whether they are poor or rich. I have a Negro friend, Willie White, for thirty-three years trainer of the Nashville ball club, who says "The world is your book, conscience is your preacher, and experience is your guide." In this same vein Jesus' teachings concerning wealth are punctuated with illustrations from life, and with appeals to both conscience and experience.

From the standpoint of our study, it is pertinent to point out that among the writers of the Synoptic Gospels Luke carries the most references, and the more substantial ones besides, on the subject of money. Quite a number of them he records along with Matthew and Mark, but the following are his alone,

1. The parable of the Rich Man and Lazarus (16:19-31).
2. The parable of the Rich Fool (12:13-21).
3. The parable of the Unrighteous Steward (16:1-13).
4. The conversion of Zacchaeus who offered to adjust his financial affairs considerably (19:1-10).
5. The brief form of the beatitude, "Blessed are you poor" with its corresponding woe, "Woe to you that are rich (6:20, 24).

By way of accounting for the fact that Luke seems to major in this area, it has been suggested that the evangelist did not care for the wealthy because he was attracted by the asceticism of the Ebionites, who placed a premium on poverty. They are a Jewish-Christian sect that held a mutilated form of Christianity, and became extinct about the fourth century. We also know that the Dead Sea Scroll Community

112

practiced *compulsory* poverty, requiring its members to donate all their earthly goods to the brotherhood. The early church in Jerusalem also made way for the sharing of property and goods, but with them it was a voluntary procedure which we may refer to as "commonism," because it states that they held all things in common. Luke tells of this latter custom in his *Acts of the Apostles.*

One does not need to conclude, however, that Luke himself espoused a specific economic theory in order to account for his inclusion of additional sayings of Jesus concerning wealth, sayings not found in Matthew and Mark. It might have been pure accident that these came to his attention. On the other hand, the possibility of his holding a particular viewpoint should not be completely dismissed. Authors tend to emphasize their preferred ideas and ideals.

Money and Providence

Basic to all that Jesus taught concerning money was his profound belief in Providence, spelled with a capital P. Among the incentives which drive men to acquire earthly goods is the fear of deprivation. In the play, *Long Day's Journey into Night,* this is made so clear as the character of Eugene O'Neill's father is presented. It was this anxiety that led our Lord to say,

> "Therefore I tell you, do not be anxious about
> your life, what you shall eat, nor about your

body, what you shall put on. For life is more than food, and the body more than clothing. Consider the ravens: they neither sow nor reap, they have neither storehouse nor barn, and yet God feeds them. Of how much more value are you than the birds! And which of you by being anxious can add a cubit to his span of life? If then you are not able to do as small a thing as that, why are you anxious about the rest? Consider the lilies, how they grow; they neither toil nor spin; yet I tell you, even Solomon in all his glory was not arrayed like one of these. But if God so clothes the grass which is alive in the field today and tomorrow is thrown into the oven, how much more will he clothe you, O men of little faith? And do not seek what you are to eat and what you are to drink, nor be of anxious mind. For all the nations of the world seek these things; and your Father knows that you need them. Instead, seek his kingdom, and these things shall be yours as well."

Luke 12:22-31

One of our problems is that we do not fully believe what this Scripture states. As a general religious truth we may give it sentimental acceptance, but as a specific fact in its relation to our daily material needs, we tend to hold reservations. And it is these reservations which are the hole in the dike of faith. It is as Sören Kierkegaard, the distinguished Danish theologian, says when he writes, "But if a man chooses to forget God, and look after his own sustenance, then he involves himself in anxiety." This is true of the rich as well as of the poor, for "If

114

the richest man that ever lives forgets God, and thinks that he is supporting himself, he has this carky anxiety. . . . Only he is spared who is content with being a man, and understands that his Heavenly Father feeds him." [1]

Jesus was thinking of this very thing in the parable of the Rich Fool (Luke 12:13-21). We find here a man who seemingly had no other faults than the belief that he should trust himself, rather than God, for his future. Rich in goods already, he wanted to be richer still. Small barns gave way to larger ones, so that he could one day say to himself, "Soul, you have ample goods laid up for many years; take your ease, eat, drink, be merry." But that day never came; death followed instead. And God called the man a fool.

In the introduction to this parable Jesus said, "A man's life does not consist in the abundance of his possessions" (12:15). This reminds us that in the wilderness of temptation our Lord decided against being an economic liberator, because men do not live by bread alone, but by the words of God. And again, in line with this same truth, he once called upon his followers to deny themselves, saying "For what does it profit a man if he gains the whole world and loses or forfeits himself?" (Luke 9:25). In all of this the emphasis is upon the fact that *life* is essentially spiritual, and that material existence is not to be substituted for it.

[1] These quotations are taken from *Meditations from Kierkegaard,* edited by T. H. Croxall (Philadelphia: The Westminster Press, copyright by W. L. Jenkins, 1955), pp. 97-98. Used by permission.

JESUS ILLUSTRATES HIS TEACHING

Jesus illustrated his great belief in Providence by the way he lived personally, as well as by the directions he gave to his disciples and immediate followers. Once when a would-be-disciple came to him and offered to join the apostolic band, Jesus said to him, "Foxes have holes, and birds of the air have nests; but the Son of man has nowhere to lay his head" (Luke 9:58). He did not have a fixed dwelling place with the material security that it affords. Like the birds and the beasts he trusted the Father on the open road.

There is no indication that Jesus plied his carpenter's trade for financial support, as the apostle Paul was later to continue his tentmaking (or working in leather) when preaching in community after community. We have one reference in Luke to the fact that some of the women who accompanied him contributed to his needs from their own means (Luke 8:3). And we learn in the Gospel of John that the group around Jesus kept a money box into which coins were placed for their daily needs (John 12:6). It is said here that it was in the keeping of Judas. Where this money came from we can only surmise. Presumably it was given to Jesus by those who were sympathetic with his work, and he regarded such gifts as coming ultimately from God himself.

In the accounts of the sending out of the twelve (Luke 9:1-6), and of the seventy (Luke 10:1-12), we read that Jesus' instructions called for the workers to carry neither purse nor wallet. They were to stay in the homes of the people who responded to their message. These procedures would accomplish two things; they would encourage the disciples to depend upon Providence, and would help the people who supported them to feel that they had a part in the work. The financial aid was in the form of a return for services rendered.

The Christian Church has, in the main, followed the guidance of Jesus here in caring for its ministers. Most religious workers are supported financially by their constituency, so that they are free from the need to earn a living in addition to their religious duties. Sometimes there have been those who have insisted that they be allowed to work at another occupation along with their preaching, for the purpose of getting close to the people. The loss here in time for spiritual preparation is often greater than the gain in rapport and camaraderie. And, of course, there are situations in which churches do not pay their ministers a living wage, so that they feel under the necessity of carrying a "second job." This is to be greatly regretted. In the instruction to the seventy did not our Lord expressly say, ". . . the laborer deserves his wages" (Luke 10:7)?

Money and Our Relation to God

Earlier in this chapter it was pointed out that Jesus has considerably more to say about money and earthly goods than is usually realized. From his teachings on this subject that we have already noted, we can begin to see his reason for this emphasis. It is related to the very definition of what man is. *Are we a body with a soul, or a soul with a body?* This is the basic question, and our answer to it will determine, to a great extent, what we think and do about money. If we place the emphasis upon the physical, our attitude toward wealth will be one thing, and if we stress first the spiritual, it will be another. Jesus, of course, emphasized the spiritual.

As our Lord pressed deeper into these concerns, he asserted over and over again the fact that our attitude toward money may affect—does invariably affect—our relationship to God. For instance, if we cry aloud with Swinburne,

> "Glory to man in the highest,
> For man is the master of things,"

we are going to place the emphasis upon our economic cleverness as we make a place for ourselves. Thus there will be no room for God in the picture. Our language gives us away at this point, does it not? When we are asked how wealthy a certain person is, we too easily reply with the colloquialism, "He is *independently* wealthy." This is a dead give-away, for it says that he needs no one, God or man. His wealth comes between himself and God.

In the Gospel of Luke are found several instances of this attitude with its tragic fruit. The story of the *Rich Young Ruler* is one example (Luke 18:18-25). Wanting the Kingdom, seeking out Jesus on his own,

118

enthusiastic about the outcome (he came running), basically religious (he had kept the commandments from his youth)—all this—and he still turned back, going away sorrowful. Why? This is the reason Luke gave: "he became sad, for he was very rich." As a condition for following him, our Lord had demanded that he give away his possessions, distributing them to the poor. This should not, however, be regarded as a universal requirement for discipleship.[2] Only when money is more important than God in the life of the individual is its renunciation required.

We can readily see that this is so in the account of the conversion of Zacchaeus, the hated tax collector (Luke 19:1-10). This is one of the narratives involving the subject of wealth, which Luke alone records. We have here another enthusiastic person —there is no substitute for zeal—who went to the length of climbing a tree to see Jesus. Our Lord invited himself to the publican's home for a meal, since Zacchaeus himself would not have felt free to do so. He probably thought Jesus regarded him as an outcast, as did the rest of the Jews. But he was gloriously mistaken.

'This must have been one of the most interesting dinner parties in history. In the presence of Jesus, Zacchaeus' life-pattern was changed. And this took some doing since he was a chief publican, a supervisor of tax collectors whose system of collection involved both extortion and dishonesty. After all,

[2] If the possession of money were wrong in itself, giving it to someone else would mean putting that person in the wrong, and could hardly be interpreted as a Christian act.

one had to make a living when the corn was green.[3]

Zacchaeus offered freely to give half of his possessions to the poor and to restore four times over what he had unlawfully taken. Jesus accepted the offer and declared that the salvation of Abraham had come to this man's house, another way of saying that it was the real thing. The difference between the Rich Young Ruler and Zacchaeus was that Zacchaeus volunteered to part with his possessions (he was not enchained by them), while the other had to be instructed to do so—and could not. Zacchaeus held his money; the Rich Young Ruler was held by his. And thus it came between himself and God, because it kept him from responding to the call of the Kingdom.

But Jesus was not insensitive to the difficulties that his teaching imposed upon the rich. Although he belonged to the poor of earth, he had an unusual ability to understand the other fellow's problem. It was this capacity for empathy that drew—and draws —persons of all classes and conditions to him. When the Rich Young Ruler turned back, Jesus said to his disciples, "How hard it is for those who have riches to enter the kingdom of God! For it is easier for a camel to go through the eye of a needle than for a rich man to enter the kingdom of God" (Luke 18:24-25).

Jesus did not say that it was impossible for a person of means to enter the Kingdom; what he did state was that it was difficult. If the situation were not so

---

[3] It has been estimated that Zacchaeus was possibly a millionaire, since he was the chief publican of the area.

weighted with tragedy, one could take time to enjoy the humor in the picture of a camel with its droll expression, eying the eye of a needle to discover a way for entry. The hyperbole of this statement, however, mirrors the struggles of the wealthy to find life eternal—as the subtle temptations of wealth threaten to smother them. But it can be done. When the disciples were discouraged at the enormity of this problem and inquired, "Who then can be saved?" Jesus said, "What is impossible with men is possible with God" (Luke 18:26-27).

One more word of Jesus should be touched upon in connection with the fact that money may come between men and God. It is a kind of summary of the problem. He once said, "No servant can serve two masters; for either he will hate the one and love the other, or he will be devoted to the one and despise the other. You cannot serve God and mammon" (Luke 16:13). The issue comes to this: Who is Lord, God or gold?

Money and Our Fellowmen

Jesus' teaching concerning money is a part of his social message, as well as being related to his concern with personal religion. The two cannot be separated. They used to say that the main point about Lincoln's humble origin was not the fact that he was born in a log cabin, but that he got out of it. And yet, he never got away from it. As he ascended in the social, political, and economic scale, he did not leave the people behind.

This is not always the case. Money often tends to keep persons apart by creating social cleavages. The big house on the hill, and the section across the tracks are all too well remembered. Although in present day suburbia there are fewer such distinctions, we still have our good and bad sections of town, based upon economic class distinctions. Lincoln would have come from one of our less desirable areas today.

Our Lord regarded barriers between persons as evil, whether they were caused by race, religion, or economics. In the kingdom of God there were to be none. One of his parables concerning earthly goods indicates how seriously he considered this matter. Usually the parable is interpreted as having to do with life after death. Its chief concern, however, is money. I refer to Luke's parable of the Rich Man and Lazarus (Luke 16:19-31). The teaching here is that if a man, through the misuse of his money, creates a gulf between himself and other people on this earth, this gulf will continue in heaven, and the miscreant will be on the wrong side of it.

You will recall how the rich man while on earth would have nothing to do with poor Lazarus. They were of different social status because of their different economic level. Lazarus attempted to bridge the gulf between them by asking for food. The rich man refused even to listen. Death came to both. Irrespective of the geography of the next world, which is not the main point in the parable, after death

Lazarus found himself seated next to Abraham at the feast of the Kingdom in heaven. The rich man (Dives) was in Hades. Neither could reach the other. There "was a great chasm" fixed between them; it had been established on earth by the rich man. His misuse of his money had determined his eternal destiny.

It must be said that with Jesus it was not money in itself that was evil; neither was having it a sin. Instead, it was the attitude which the possession of wealth sometimes created which was the crux of the matter. Persons, not pocketbooks, were the issue. Money brought temptations that the lack of it did not create.

BLESSED ARE YOU POOR

On the other hand, not having enough money can demoralize people. Lack of money can bring about malnutrition, physical harm, and other attendant evils. It can also dull men's moral sensibilities. Jean Valjeans* will invariably be tempted to steal bread when starving. And in the modern world there are more refined ways of stealing this than ransacking a shop.

Not having money to meet one's economic needs may also cause a person to regard wealth as the answer to everything. But even millionaires sometimes shoot themselves. Even so, the poor, just as much as the wealthy, may worship gold instead of

* Victor Hugo, *Les Misérables.*

God. Economics, morality, and the development of man's spiritual being are so intricately intertwined in our daily experience that the attempt to assess any one factor in the situation must include consideration of all three. When I was in college the professors in the economics departments were the social prophets on the campus. They were not concerned primarily with their theories, as such, but with a better life for persons, the poor and the rich alike. This was always Jesus' point of view.

Our Lord rejoiced that the gospel was preached to the poor (Luke 7:22), but he did not hold a bias against the man who was rich (Mark 10:21). Both counted for eternity in the sight of his heavenly Father. He believed that the good news of the Kingdom would deliver the poor from feeling that they were of little value, that is, from their feeling of inferiority. This is, in part, the meaning of the beatitude, "Blessed are you poor." At the same time, the gospel would help the rich to realize what was the true wealth and give them a sense of responsibility for their needy brothers.

BLESSED ARE YOU RICH

Our discussion should close on a positive note. Although in the Beatitudes one does not find the words, "Blessed are you rich," they are not contrary to Jesus' total teaching concerning earthly goods. In fact, they are implied in such a parable as that of the Unrighteous Steward (Luke 16:1-13). Here we see a clever man who used his brains to assure himself economic security. When he tampered with his master's accounts receivable, so that those whom he thus favored would care for him after he was fired from his job as steward, Jesus expressed admiration. Speaking of this rascal, he said that "the sons of this world are wiser in their own generation than the sons of light" (Luke 16:8).

We are not to conclude that our Lord approved of the steward's dishonesty. Not at all! Had the story been continued, no doubt, he would have told of the crook's arrest. But he was impressed by his foresight. Knowing that he was to be dismissed, he did something to safeguard his future. Why did not religious people similarly use their creative imaginations? Why did they not look ahead and apply as much intelligence in the cause of righteousness as evil men did in the cause of sin? It is a pathetic question, but very pointed.

Then Jesus added these words, "And I tell you, make friends for yourselves by means of unrighteous mammon, so that when it fails they may receive you into the eternal habitations" (Luke 16:9). Here is an invitation to turn money into the coin of the realm, God's realm. It can be made to support the causes of the Kingdom, so that the result is not material wealth, but education, health, proper housing, brotherhood, and the spread of the gospel. The Christian ought to know what to do with money and how to spend it so that it will contribute to spiritual values.

Final Days—The Cross

THE ACCOUNT OF THE CROSS was probably the first of the stories about Jesus to be put into writing. Many think that it circulated separately before it was included in a Gospel. There can be no doubt but that it was the most moving of all the events in his life—the most moving and the most baffling. Men have pointed to it as an indication that there is no God, at least not a good God. He would not have allowed the Crucifixion to happen if he had existed. On the other hand, some have looked at the cross and found God there in the depths of the love revealed in Jesus' sacrifice of himself.

Paul once spoke of the cross as being a stumbling block to the Jews (I Corinthians 1:23). It was also this at first to the Jewish-Christians. The Law (Deuteronomy 21:22-23) had pronounced any person who was hanged on a tree as accursed. Yet the followers of Jesus were proclaiming him as the Messiah. What a situation! The contradiction was resolved, however, by the interpretation of the Crucifixion in terms of the prophecy concerning the Suffering Servant in Isaiah 52:13—53:12. He died for love of others. "With his stripes we are healed." We have seen that there is reason to believe that Jesus himself applied these Scriptures to his coming death.[1] They gave meaning and purpose to an experience which otherwise was stark tragedy.

The early church could not present its message to the world until it was able to face and fathom the mystery of the cross. This fact contributed to the need to formulate the account of the Crucifixion at the outset and in all likelihood this is what was done.

The Synoptic Gospels paint essentially the same picture of the last days of Jesus' life in Jerusalem. This includes such happenings as the Triumphal Entry, the Cleansing of the Temple, the conflict with the religious leaders of the Jews, the Discourse on Last Things and the End of the Age, the betrayal by Judas, the Last Supper, Gethsemane, the arrest, trial, and Crucifixion, and the Resurrection. There are variations in emphasis, however, as each writer records his account. This is what we would expect with different authorship. In addition, some are familiar with sayings and actions not known by the others. For instance, it requires statements from four of the Gospels to make up the list of the last words from the cross. No single one records all seven. This

[1] See p. 57.

is a further illustration of what we referred to in chapter one as "the gospel according to you."

Luke Tells His Story

It is with Luke's individual touches in presenting the account of our Lord's last days in Jerusalem that we are particularly concerned in this chapter. In general, these may be said to take the reader more intimately into the feelings of the persons involved than, for instance, the Gospel of Mark. Luke's understanding of human emotions and motivation make him more than a simple chronicler of events; he is historian, interpreter, and dramatist. In addition, he is an evangelist who is as eager to proclaim the message of the cross as he is to record its details.

THE TRIUMPHAL ENTRY

Prior to presenting the account of the Triumphal Entry, Luke gives an extended narrative of the Perean Ministry of Jesus on the eastern side of the Jordan (9:51 through 18:30). It covers the last journey to Jerusalem from Capernaum.[2] Although in all probability Jesus made such a trek, Luke builds into it a dramatic last appeal to the Gentiles, and includes

[2] In the *Acts of the Apostles* Luke also presents a last journey to Jerusalem for the apostle Paul. He gives to it the same dramatic feeling that we find in his account of Jesus' final journey to the Holy City.

materials that are found in an entirely different context in the other Gospels. Some of the teachings are reminiscent of the Sermon on the Mount. Pharisees also appear in conflict with Jesus during these days. And, in addition, there is a deliberate attempt to prepare the disciples for the hour when he will be taken from them. This is high drama with developing suspense as the Holy City comes into view.

The Triumphal Entry is recognized in the New Testament as Jesus' public announcement that he is the Messiah. Although he does not mount a horse of war, choosing instead an humble ass, he nevertheless rides in the majesty of a King. The plaudits of the pilgrims who were en route to the Passover Feast proclaim him as such. He comes "in the name of the Lord." Luke, in particular, describes the reactions of the people. He says that they "began to rejoice and praise God with a loud voice for all the mighty works that they had seen" (Luke 19:37).

Our evangelist is also impressed with the intensity of feeling that Jesus experienced at this time. When the Pharisees attempted to quell the outburst of the people, he says that Jesus replied, "I tell you that, if these were silent, the very stones would cry out." (Luke 19:40). *This recognition of the Christ had to be made.* The universe itself was behind it. There could be no stopping it; God himself through nature would announce it if men refused or were hindered.

Still caught up in the reaction of Jesus personally to this significant moment, Luke interrupts the narrative as Mark and Matthew present it at this point to record that when the Lord drew nigh unto the city he wept over it, because it did not know the "things that make for peace." He announced that the days would come when it would be a besieged city that would be finally destroyed. All this would happen because they knew not the time of God's visitation (Luke 19:41-44). The drama of this situation has never been more vividly noted than in Luke's account of what Jesus said.

THE CLEANSING OF THE TEMPLE

The cleansing of the Temple was the culmination of the conflict between Jesus and the religious leaders of the Jews. Its coming at the beginning of the last week in Jerusalem is significant, for it marked the final act which decided his enemies that he should be killed. Although, to instruct his readers in the purpose and mission of Christ, the author of John's Gospel places the event at the beginning of our Lord's ministry,[3] its proper place is probably where we find it in Luke and the other Synoptics. What we know about Jesus and his methods of teaching and working would suggest that this kind of dramatic deed would more likely come as a climax to his ministry, rather than as an opening volley.

The purpose of this show of strength was prophetic instead of personal. Jesus' anger was always of this kind. He did not strike back in retaliation because of

[3] The position it is given in the Fourth Gospel enables the author to dramatize his conviction that Jesus was superior to the old order he was replacing. Some scholars (Garvie *et al.*), however, contend that it occurred twice.

131

what persons did to him as an individual. Instead, when he felt incensed it was because of what was being done to others. It was the same with the use of his power. He did not turn to it to deliver himself from difficult situations, but employed it only in the service of the people in need.[4]

The prophetic character of the cleansing lay in Jesus' zeal for pure worship. This was being denied by the priests because of the religious system at the Temple, with its formal and pedantic regulations and requirements. The words that Jesus spoke at this time have their roots in two Old Testament passages which stress the opportunities for worship and the sin of denying it (Isaiah 56:7 and Jeremiah 7:11). "It is written, 'My house shall be a house of prayer;' but you have made it a den of robbers" (Luke 19: 46), he said to those who were selling the animals for sacrifice. All this interfered with communion with God, therefore those who were promoting it were "robbing" the people of their opportunity to pray.

Luke omits the reference to the money changers and the overthrowing of the tables of exchange, although he must surely have been familiar with it, for it appears prominently in Mark (11:15). This means that there is less violence in his account. Could he have felt that too much stress was being placed upon this side of the event, and that it was becoming an incentive to acts of aggression in his (Luke's) own day? We know that the cleansing has

[4] A possible exception may be found in the account of the Sermon at Nazareth with its tragic aftermath (Luke 4:16-30), but even here the details are lacking so that it is difficult to draw a final conclusion.

been used by some moderns as an argument to justify war.

Or, could it have been that Luke omitted the reference to the destruction of the tables because he did not want to give substance to the false charge of some of his contemporaries that the Christians were violent opposers, and that they would not support the Roman state? [5] By focusing largely upon the physical act, it would have been easy to have constructed a misleading picture of Jesus, building him up as an insurrectionist who would overthrow established order, even in matters of religion. With the full story before us, we know that it was not the material factors that were central here. It is to be lamented, however, that even today, in interpreting this event, too much emphasis is sometimes placed upon them. We need Luke's perspective.

There is an additional individualistic touch by Luke in his account of the Cleansing of the Temple which should be noted. It, too, is in line with his interest in showing that Jesus was not an anti-institutionalist, as such. After recording that our Lord had cleansed the Temple, he says that "he was teaching daily in the temple" (Luke 19:47). He did not remain aloof; he was not one of the persons who would stay away from church because he did not like the preacher or approve of the order of service. It was God's house, and he would remain loyal to it, even though he would not hesitate to point out the weaknesses in its practice.

[5] See the previous reference to this background, pp. 10-11.

It is difficult to envision fully the events in the life of our Lord during the last week in Jerusalem. The following assignment of days and major events is usually made:

Sunday—The Triumphal Entry

Monday—The Cleansing of the Temple

Tuesday—A Day of Teaching and Conflict

Wednesday—A Day of Rest Outside Jerusalem

Thursday—The Last Supper

Friday—The Crucifixion

Saturday—In the Tomb

Sunday—The Resurrection

In the face of the nature of the records covering these days, an outline such as this should be regarded as tentative. For instance, it is not clear whether the last day of Jesus' public ministry was Tuesday or Wednesday. So many teachings are crowded into this period, without any indication of time, that it is difficult to place them definitely.

Mark's order of events covering the last week should probably be given here, because it is basic to all of the accounts. The Jerusalem ministry in Matthew lasted but two days. In Luke the division into days is not emphasized. Here is the Markan order with the sequence of happenings as he knew them:

> "Immediately after the Triumphal Entry, Jesus visited briefly the Temple and returned to

134

Bethany that same evening (11:11). En route to Jerusalem the next day he noticed a fig tree without fruit and cursed it (11:12-14). Upon his arrival in the city he cleansed the Temple, driving out those who bought and sold within its sacred precincts (11:15-18). That night he left Jerusalem again, going (presumably) to Bethany (11:19). The day following on their way to Jerusalem, Jesus and his party passed the fig tree, and notice was taken of the fact that it had withered (11:20-25). Once again Jesus went to the Temple, where open argument with the religious leaders followed (11:27—12:40). Jesus observed, also, the sacrificial giving of the widow who placed her mite in the offering box (12:41-44). He predicted then the destruction of the Temple (13:1-2). Later, sitting on the Mount of Olives, Jesus spoke at length concerning the end of the age (13:3-37). At this juncture Mark says that it was two days before the Passover, and tells of the anointing of Jesus at Bethany, and of the arrangements Judas made to betray him (14:1-11). This is followed by the account of the Last Supper 'on the day of Unleavened Bread, when they sacrificed the passover lamb' (14:12-25). The prayer retreat in Gethsemane, the arrest, the trial, and the Crucifixion are next presented (14:26-15:47), leading up to the Resurrection (16:1-8)." [6]

[6] See the author's *Life and Teachings of Jesus,* p. 272.

Luke's account parallels Mark's with a few exceptions. He does not include the story of the withered fig tree, nor the parable of the Marriage Feast. Following the discourse on Last Things which he presents along with Matthew and Mark, he gives in typical fashion a personal warning of Jesus against being unprepared for the Day of Judgment (Luke 21:34-36). He does not tell of the anointing of Jesus at Bethany.

These were days of intense effort on Jesus' part. He was faced with the need to meet the issue that the religious system of his day presented. The definition of differences here is clear and unforgettable. There was no escaping the necessity of sharpening the line, for a part of his mission as the Messiah was to challenge prophetically the false practices of official Judaism at that time. Again, our Lord had to keep the populace in mind. His main teaching to them had already been given, but they remained his chief concern, and they were numerous in Jerusalem during this period of the Passover. Finally, there were the Twelve who were in such a precipitous position. They were caught up in events beyond their present understanding. So much in the days ahead depended upon them.

JUDAS—THE BETRAYAL

We took note at the outset of this chapter that Luke focuses upon the personal factors in the record of these last days in the life of our Lord. We can see this in his consideration of the betrayal of Jesus by Judas. Although Matthew and Luke carry accounts of this disciple's defection, Luke adds some interpretive touches that are revealing. He says that "Satan entered into Judas called Iscariot, who was of the number of the twelve" (Luke 22:3). Furthermore, he states that the betrayer agreed and sought opportunity to deliver Jesus to the rulers "in the absence of the multitude."

I have no disposition to build up these insights of Luke into major proportions. But they do suggest that Luke was troubled, not only by the fact that Judas betrayed Jesus, but also with the questions of why he did it, and how he could have done such a dark deed. Our evangelist is like us in this respect, for these are our inquiries too. We have asked them over and over again. The answer Luke gives is that Satan *entered* into the life of Judas, and that this disciple *allowed* him to do so. He *consented* to the plan.

Attempts have been made to understand Judas' act by suggesting that he was only trying to force Jesus to declare himself as the King, and to set up his rule at once. He placed him in a position where he would have to do so, or else lose his life. Luke would not have accepted this view. To him evil was very real. It was spelled with a capital "E," and its source was Satan. Judas gave him entrance; this was his sin. One wonders sometimes whether our psychological approaches to sin are not a bit sentimental and unrealistic. Whether or not we believe in a personal devil, we must accept the reality of temptation, and assume responsibility for making right choices, and face the dread consequences of our sin in the sight of man and God.

THE LAST SUPPER

In presenting the Last Supper, Luke again enters understandingly and uniquely into the tradition he is

137

recording. He alone among the Synoptic authors notes that on this occasion Jesus said "I have earnestly desired to eat this passover with you before I suffer" (Luke 22:15). This meal was important to Jesus personally; he coveted a final opportunity with the disciples. Luke adds, also, that Jesus referred to the coming of the Kingdom, saying "I shall not eat it (the Passover) until it is fulfilled in the kingdom of God" (Luke 22:16). In spite of the fact that the King was to be killed, our Lord's personal faith in the advent of the kingdom of God held firm. Along with Matthew and Mark, Luke then proceeds to tell of the establishing of the Lord's Supper.

Yet another special touch in Luke's recital of what occurred about the table at the Last Supper is his inclusion of the word concerning Peter. After telling the disciples that they had been with him in his temptations, he turned to Peter and, with both kindness and firmness, warned him of the battle with temptation that he would have. Satan would seek to sift him like wheat. But Jesus expressed confidence in Peter's eventual loyalty. He had prayed for him and anticipated that, although he would deny him, Peter would return to his former stanchness. Not only this; he would also become the stay and strength of the others (Luke 22:31-32).

There is one further word of Jesus which only Luke carries on this momentous occasion. It looks to the future and envisions the personal needs of the disciples as they attempted to bear their witness to the Kingdom. Our Lord reminded them of their earlier missionary tours, and of the instruction he had given at that time. No purse, nor wallet, nor shoes were allowed them then. *But now*—now it was different! Times had changed; the opposition would be cruel and desperate. Therefore, not only purses and wallets, but also a sword, even if it were necessary to sell one's cloak to purchase it (Luke 22:35-38).

We should not make the mistake of being crassly literal here. When one of the disciples suddenly produced two swords, brandishing them excitedly in the air, Jesus quickly said "It is enough," or "Enough! Enough!" (Moffatt). What he meant was "Too much! Too much!" They were not getting the point. He was intending to tell them that they should be alert and forearmed for any and all situations. But they could only think of defending themselves against attack. This was probably because they were worried and unsure of what the morrow would bring. The clouds hung heavily over the horizon of their future.

GETHSEMANE

Jesus was arrested in the Garden of Gethsemane where he had gone with his disciples from the Upper Room. Hallowed by the words spoken and emotions felt, this sanctuary has been sacred to Christians through the centuries. It was the praying of Jesus that we remember most, the praying to be delivered from the necessity of drinking the cup. Although our Lord had already dedicated himself to death on the cross, he would not rush into crucifixion with sentimental fanaticism. Only if his martyrdom were essential in carrying out God's purpose would it possess moral reality; if there were some other way, the cross would not have been the right way.

And so he prayed, "Father, if thou art willing, remove this cup from me." It was a proper prayer and natural. But this is not the reason for its greatness. Other words followed which make it peculiarly Jesus' prayer, the expression of his mind and heart: "Nevertheless not my will, but thine be done" (Luke 22:42). These words were not a sentiment of the moment. They represented our Lord's constant attitude toward God. *Because he lived the will of his Father daily, he could pray for that will in the crisis hour.* Remember how he taught his disciples to pray "Thy will be done on earth as it is in heaven"? He was applying this prayer to his own life in its most difficult decision.

As before, Luke captures the inner, personal side of the situation, and enters feelingly into the soul of Jesus. He alone tells us that, "being in an agony he [Jesus] prayed more earnestly; and his sweat became like great drops of blood falling down upon the ground" (Luke 22:44). Was Luke's description that of the literary artist attempting to capture the human interest in the scene? Or was it Luke the Christian who, having himself been "crucified with Christ," was sensitive to the heartbreak of his Lord? Surely it must have been both. The evangelist also tells us that an angel from heaven appeared to Jesus and strengthened him (Luke 22:43).

140

Matthew and Mark report that Jesus prayed the prayer to be delivered from the cup three times. Luke gives us but one offering of it. Perhaps he concluded that this was sufficient to represent adequately the issue. Or, could it have been that he felt it so deeply himself as he wrote the words, that a single reporting was all he could manage? Who can say?

There is a further word of Jesus in the Garden which Luke alone presents. It too is very intimate, as the others have been. Like Matthew and Mark, he knows that Judas had agreed upon a kiss as the sign by which he would point Jesus out to the Temple guards. But when the kiss is about to be given, Luke notes that Jesus interfered and said to him, "Judas, would you betray the Son of man *with a kiss?*" [7] The most personal of all human acts, the sign of discipleship and of love itself, should not be prostituted to the level of rejection and betrayal. [8] What irony! What infamy!

THE TRIAL

We have been looking at the last days in the life of our Lord through the eyes and pen of Luke. Again and again we have discovered the unique insight he shows in recording the tradition which he possessed. Some of this special character is due to the fact that he had in his collection certain data which Matthew and Mark did not know. Another contributing cause,

[7] Italics are the author's.
[8] See Luke 22:49. In Mark 14:45 the kiss was actually given.

however, is his own sensitivity to the concerns of persons. He knows how they feel from the inside, and therefore he is able to sense what is pertinent.

We can see this quality in Luke's account of the trial of Jesus. In the main he follows the sequence in Mark rather closely. First, our Lord is taken before a special session of the Jewish authorities. Then he is brought before Pilate. The charge before the former body was largely religious: that of blasphemy,[9] based on his claim that he was God's Son. The accusations presented at Pilate's court, however, are civil and political. "Did he, or did he not claim to be the King of the Jews?" is the question that is asked.

Our evangelist is at his best in describing these events. He does not miss the drama of the situation for a single moment. And, as elsewhere, he shows penetrating insight in his use of material not found in the other Gospels. For instance, he details three charges which the Jews leveled against Jesus in Pilate's court. They are so pertinent to the issue that we should surely be poorer if we did not have them. It was claimed that (1) Jesus perverted the nation, (2) forbade the paying of taxes to Caesar, and (3) set himself up as a king in opposition to the emperor (Luke 23:2). It is difficult to see how Matthew and Mark could have missed these. Perhaps they knew them but passed them by. Luke, however, saw in them the insincerity of our Lord's accusers. No one with any knowledge of Jesus at all would have paid them any heed. They were obviously false, and, as

[9] Blasphemy was a religious crime, punishable by death under the Mosaic Law.

such, revealed the inner motives of his enemies. It is remarkable that Luke recorded these charges, since he was interested in showing the Roman world that the Christians were not insurrectionists, and could be loyal to the government (see *Text*, page 11).

This concern for presenting the followers of Jesus as guiltless of political duplicity, shows itself in Luke's account through the representation of Pilate as one who was convinced of our Lord's innocency. More than in the other Synoptics, the Third Gospel stresses the governor's interest in releasing him. He does not wish to pass sentence, so that when he learns that Jesus was of Herod's jurisdiction, he sends his prisoner to appear before the king (Luke 23:7-12). When the ruler returned him unsentenced, Pilate attempts to secure his release by offering to chastise him. This should satisfy his accusers—but it did not. At one point Luke says that Pilate actually desired to release Jesus; at another he notes that the procurator (this was the third attempt to let our Lord go free) actually inquired of the Jews, "Why, what evil has he done? I have found in him no crime deserving death" (Luke 23:22). But it was to no avail, and finally their voices prevailed. As they had requested, he freed Barabbas and delivered Jesus over to be crucified.

The Crucifixion

The Crucifixion is presented in the Synoptics with remarkable objectivity. Their authors do not pause

143

to weep as they write, although their hearts are deeply moved. Even Luke, who has shown such a tendency to enter personally into the events he describes, exhibits unusual restraint. And here, again, he has his own materials. He alone tells of the weeping of the women who followed the cross on its way to Golgotha (Luke 23:27-31). We have noted already that Luke shows a special interest in the place Jesus made for women in the kingdom movement, therefore, we are not surprised to discover this story in his recital of the Crucifixion. Our Lord turns to the women and says, "Daughters of Jerusalem, do not weep for me, but weep for yourselves and for your children." Then he predicts the judgment of God upon a nation that would reject the true Messiah, commenting "For if they do this when the wood is green, what will happen when it is dry?"

Of the seven last words of Jesus from the cross, Luke records three not found elsewhere in the Gospels. They are the prayer for the forgiveness of his enemies: "Father, forgive them; for they know not what they do" (Luke 23:34); the promise of new life in heaven for the repentant thief: "Truly, I say to you, today you will be with me in Paradise" (Luke 23:43); and the prayer of commitment by which our Lord gave himself into the keeping of God: "Father, into thy hands I commit my spirit!" (Luke 23:46). This latter word, Luke states, Jesus uttered, crying with a loud voice.

When it was all over, our evangelist, once again entering into the souls of the persons who were caught up in these events, states, "And all the multitudes who assembled to see the sight, *when they saw what had taken place*,[10] returned home beating their breasts." (Luke 23:48). Some, perchance, had come out of curiosity. There were always hangers-on at crucifixions. But they, too, had returned, deeply stirred. And well they might have been.

[10] Italics are the author's.

C
H
A
P
T
E
R X

The Resurrected Life═══

THE PLACE TO BEGIN a consideration of the Resurrection is with the experience of the Living Christ which Christians have known down through the centuries to this very hour. Unless we comprehend the reality of the Resurrection, today, through our personal experience with the Living Christ, we shall not be able to grasp the meaning of the Resurrection as a historical truth. For it is faith and experience, rather than objective analysis and the technical study of documents, which confirm the resurrection stories. Let me say it another way. To read the accounts of the Resurrection outside of the experience of the Church is one thing, but to read them within the warmth and fellowship of the Christian community is quite a different thing. It is the difference between knowing and KNOWING.

The Gospels Bear Witness

The Gospels themselves should be read as the testimony of the Church. Believers wrote them, not doubters. Their authors were talking about themselves and their own experiences as they penned the record. Luke was not one of the original witnesses to the Resurrection, but he belonged to the resurrection fellowship. Therefore when he spoke of Peter, the women, the Emmaus pair, and the disciples, he was one of them and knew personally what they meant when they said they had seen the Risen Lord.

Much is sometimes made of the divergencies in the Synoptic accounts of the Resurrection. Mark relates only a Judean appearance;[1] Matthew and Luke include a Galilean. In Mark it is a young man within the tomb who informs the women that Jesus has risen, while Luke says that there were two young men in dazzling apparel, and Matthew states that it was an angel. Luke includes a lengthy story of Jesus' appearance to the two who were journeying to Emmaus which neither Mark nor Matthew narrates. These are typical differences in detail among the Synoptic Gospels. If we were to include the resurrection narratives in the Gospel of John and the list of appearances in Paul's recital in First Corin-

[1] The end of Mark's account is missing, but he does report that Jesus said he would meet the disciples in Galilee. Mark 16:9-20 appears in the King James Version, but it is not in the best manuscripts and has probably been added from another source. The Revised Standard Version carries it as a footnote.

thians, there would be still variations to point out.

These divergencies are what we would expect in the reporting of an experience such as the Resurrection. The story of the Resurrection was too stupendous in character, too broad in its setting, and too varied in the types of persons involved in its narration to be free from inconsistencies. Had the accounts been without variation we should suspect that someone had tampered with them. Throughout this book we have noted that Luke made his own approach to the portrait of Christ within the general pattern of the accepted tradition. When we come to his narration of the Resurrection the same is true.

In passing, we should not forget that the earliest written account of the Resurrection is to be found in First Corinthians (15:3-11). And Paul declares that his list of appearances came to him from others. Although he does not name these persons, he was personally acquainted with some of those who had first met the living Christ, and it was probably they who told him. Paul included himself among those to whom our Lord revealed his presence. He was in all likelihood referring to his Damascus Road experience (Acts 9, 22, 26), which we customarily speak of as the occasion of his conversion to Christianity.

Appearances with a Meaning

There is an aura of mystery in the events which involve the resurrection appearances of Jesus. But

Luke's straightforward statement in his Acts of the Apostles that "he presented himself alive after his passion by many proofs, appearing to them during forty days, and *speaking of the kingdom of God*" [2] (Acts 1:3), helps us in this regard. Luke's account removes the Resurrection from the area of the occult and gives it meaning. This is to say that Jesus' appearances were not of the sort usually associated with a seance, not a hit-or-miss now-you-see-me-now-you-don't affair. They were a continuation of the preaching ministry of our Lord. He spoke to them, Luke says, of the kingdom of God. This was the theme of his earthly ministry; it was also the concern of his post-resurrection ministry.

Among the writers of the Synoptic Gospels it is Luke who seems particularly to have captured this truth, although it is not completely missing in Matthew and Mark. Luke's resurrection narratives seem to major in *the message* of the Risen Lord. Christ has a teaching to announce beyond the fact that he has risen from the dead, although this in itself carries its own divine Word. Some of you will recall *Time Marches On,* the title of a motion picture series, the precursor of the documentary film. A title which could well be applied to the meaning and message of the Resurrection might read, *The Kingdom Marches On.*

First of all, the Resurrection was personally upsetting to the disciples. They did not know how to accept it. We read that they were both fearful and

<hr>

[2] Italics are the author's.

joyous, and that they trembled with astonishment. Amazement was the predominant mood of the hour —and well it might have been. But a person cannot build for the future on amazement alone. This mood must settle down into a pattern of meaning, or it will be only an emotional outburst. We are not surprised, therefore, to discover that the Risen Jesus sought to establish a perspective in which his resurrection could be understood.

The Emmaus Revelation

Luke's narrative of the journey to Emmaus should be understood in the light of this purpose (Luke 24:13-32). More than any of the other accounts it interprets the meaning of this transcendent event. We see two persons traveling to a small community that is said to be about seven miles from Jerusalem. They were filled with consternation as they discussed the recent events that surrounded the Crucifixion and the Resurrection. While they considered these matters they were joined by a Third Person whom they did not recognize. Luke states that "their eyes were kept from recognizing him." It is suggestive to recall that Mary Magdalene, likewise, did not know at first that the one to whom she was talking near the tomb was the resurrected Jesus; she thought him to be the gardener (John 20:11-18).

Why this confusion in identity? The answer must be sought within the character of the appearances themselves, and their immediate purpose. For instance, it was best for the two travelers not to know that it was Jesus with whom they were walking. Under the circumstances they were more free to unburden their hearts and to think of what he was saying. Had they known, they would have been overpowered with wonder. And in the case of the Magdalene, tears may have so filled her eyes that her vision was dimmed, and grief may have so dulled her mind that perception was difficult.

The first thing Jesus did in speaking to the two on the road was to inquire concerning the subject of their conversation. This would provide a foundation for the teaching he was to give. They told him of Jesus of Nazareth whom they described as "a prophet mighty in deed and word before God and all the people" (Luke 24:19). This one had been delivered up to be condemned to death by the chief priests and rulers. Then they added wistfully, "But we had hoped that he was the one to redeem Israel" (24: 21). The expectations of the Jews for centuries past were in these words. Prophets and seers alike had longed for the day when the Messiah would come. These two, along with others, thought that it had arrived, but the Crucifixion intervened. However, reports of the Resurrection were in the air. Some women had found an empty tomb and had seen a vision of angels. What could it mean?

The way was now open for Jesus to explain the meaning of the Resurrection. So "beginning with Moses and all the prophets, he interpreted to them

in all the scriptures the things concerning himself"
(24:27). And central in this interpretation was the
fact that "it was necessary that the Christ should
suffer these things and enter into his glory" (24:26).
The point here is that the Resurrection was not
simply a resuscitation from death, startling as this
would have been. What was more important was
that it was a part of God's redemptive work carried
on through the ages, beginning as far back as Moses.
Therefore, it does not stand out as an isolated event,
as a kind of cosmic spectacular. The Resurrection
belongs to the deepest movement of divine revelation. God is at work through it. As Paul was later to
say when writing to the Romans, Jesus was "des-
ignated Son of God in power according to the Spirit
of holiness by his resurrection from the dead" (Romans 1:4).

Luke tells of a later appearance of Jesus to the
eleven disciples, and those who were with them, at
Jerusalem (Luke 24:36-49). Here again he calls
their attention to the things he had said to them
when present in the flesh, namely, "that everything
written about me in the law of Moses and the
prophets and the psalms must be fulfilled" (24:44).
We cannot stress too forcibly the conviction of the
earliest Christian community which shines through
these words, and is, in part, based upon them, that
the events in the life of Jesus, including his death and
resurrection, were of God.

The story of Christ is not a human tale of passing
significance only. The very meaning of existence
itself is made known in its events.

A Call to the Future

The Resurrection not only looked to God's revelation in the past. It also pointed toward his purposes in the future. "Repentance and forgiveness of sins should be preached in his [Jesus'] name to all nations, beginning from Jerusalem" (Luke 24:47). This is Luke's version of Matthew's Great Commission in which the Risen Lord says: "Go therefore and make disciples of all nations, baptizing them in the name of the Father and of the Son and of the Holy Spirit, teaching them to observe all that I have commanded you; and *lo, I am with you always, to the close of the age*" [3] (Matthew 28:19-20).

We should note how Matthew's text relates the Resurrection to the mission of the Church. We are not called upon to evangelize the world by ourselves and in our own strength. Christ, the living Lord, is with us. And as we proclaim him, he proclaims himself through us. The Resurrection is perpetuated as the Church fulfills its task.

It was for this reason that Luke felt compelled to write the book of Acts. The Resurrection made it necessary because it was not the cessation, no matter how glorious, of God's revelation in Christ, but the beginning of future manifestations. By it the Crucifixion was transformed from a dead-end street into an arterial highway into all the tomorrows. As I have written elsewhere:

[3] Italics are the author's.

154

"The Resurrection is pivoted in this total New Testament portrait of Christ. Jesus' earthly ministry is viewed in the light of the resurrection fact, and his continuing career as Christ the Lord is seen also as stemming from this same transcendent event. To separate the two would have been unthinkable to a New Testament author, including the writers of the Gospels. While all regarded the human life of Jesus as real, they were certain that his total significance for faith could not be limited to his pre-resurrection ministry." [4]

The point here is that it was the Resurrection, followed by the Ascension, that revealed Jesus of Nazareth to be Christ the Lord. As Lord, he leads his Church down the corridors of time, in our own day no less than in the past.

CONDITIONS AND SIGNS OF HIS PRESENCE

One of the questions which is frequently asked is "How can I tell when the Living Christ is present?" It is a sound inquiry, for we may take too much for granted when we speak of it. Luke's account of the appearance of Jesus to the two on the Emmaus road is revealing at this point. It indicates both the conditions and the signs of his presence.

First of all, the Lord joined himself to them while they were thinking of him. Their minds were filled with the events that had occurred. This meant that

[4] See the author's *Christ in the New Testament,* p. 13.

they were not preoccupied with a multiplicity of other matters. There was room for him in the inn of their thoughts. This, it seems to me, is basic to a realization of the presence of Christ.

In the second place, their thinking of Christ was meaningful because it was based upon certain facts with which they were familiar. They knew about his teachings and his deeds of mercy. I would not say that our Lord has not revealed himself to those who lacked a knowledge of his life and teachings, but I do sincerely believe that the person who is informed about Christ is most likely to be conscious of his presence. It is for this reason that Christian nurture is of such great importance.

In the third place they needed him, and knew that they did. They were discouraged, if not actually despondent, because their hopes in Jesus had been dashed to earth by the Crucifixion. And even the reports of the women that the grave was empty had only added to their consternation. So many possibilities were involved. It was bewildering, to say the least. But our Lord seems to find a ready access into our lives when we are in particular need of him. When sorrow and disappointment have softened our souls, we are more open to receive him.

Finally, it should also be noted that Christ revealed himself to the two as they sat about the table in their humble home. They were sharing their food with a stranger; hospitality was there, and loving fellowship besides. They had even invited him to do the honors and break the bread. It was the same with the cobbler whom Edwin Markham enshrined in his poem.[5] He had waited all day for Christ to keep his promise that he would visit him. And the fare he had prepared to share with the King, he had given to those in need who had come to his door. But Christ did not appear—or so he thought. That night, however, the Lord told him that he had come; in the persons of the visitors who had entered his shop, the Christ had been present.

As for the signs of Christ's presence, Luke's account of the Emmaus Journey is also enlightening. For one thing, as he walked with them the Scriptures took on a new meaning. Whenever the Bible comes alive for us, it is rather good evidence that Christ is at hand. Because of this, every great revival in history has been Bible-centered. As the Scriptures spoke to Christ during the days of his flesh, so Christ speaks through the Scriptures to those who follow him, then and now. This is not a preachment; it is a fact of experience.

There was yet another sign of Christ's presence in Luke's narrative. It was the burning heart that the men experienced. They said to each other as they made their way back to Jerusalem to tell of their encounter, "Did not our hearts burn within us while he talked to us on the road?" Moses had found God in the burning bush; these two had discovered Christ in the burning heart. And did not our own John

[5] Edwin Markham. "How the Great Guest Came," from *The Best Loved Poems of the American People*, selected by Hazel Felleman (New York: Garden City Publishing Co., 1936), pp. 296-297.

Wesley refer to his conversion as a time when he felt that his heart was strangely warmed? When the Risen Lord is near we can discern his presence in our hearts. No one need inform us; the soul has its own way of knowing.

Books for Further Study

The carefully selected books listed below may be borrowed from your pastor's, public or college library, or ordered from The Methodist Publishing House serving your territory.

General New Testament Studies

BALY, DENIS. *The Geography of the Bible.* New York: Harper & Bros., 1957.

BARNETT, ALBERT E. *The New Testament: Its Making and Meaning.* Nashville: Abingdon Press, 1946.

BARNETT, ALBERT E. *Understanding the Parables of Our Lord.* Naperville, Ill.: Alec R. Allenson, 1954.

BURTON, ERNEST DE WITT, and EDGAR J. GOODSPEED. *A Harmony of the Synoptic Gospels for Historical and Critical Study.* New York: Chas. Scribner's Sons, c. 1945.

BUTTRICK, GEORGE A., ed. *The Interpreter's Bible,* VII-XII. Nashville: Abingdon Press, 1951-1957.

CADBURY, HENRY J. "The New Testament and Early Christian Literature," *The Interpreter's Bible,* VII, 32-42. Nashville: Abingdon Press, 1951.

CROSS, FRANK MOORE, JR. *The Ancient Library of Qumran and Modern Biblical Studies.* Garden City: Doubleday & Co., 1958.

DANA, H. E. *The New Testament World.* 3rd rev. ed. Nashville: Broadman Press, 1946.

FILSON, FLOYD V. *The Origins of the Gospels.* Nashville: Abingdon Press, 1938. (Out of print.)

GOODSPEED, EDGAR J. *An Introduction to the New Testament.* Chicago: The University of Chicago Press, 1937.

GRANT, FREDERICK C. *An Introduction to New Testament Thought.* Nashville: Abingdon Press, 1950.

GRANT, FREDERICK C. *The Economic Background of the Gospels.* London: Oxford University Press, 1926.

GRANT, FREDERICK C. *The Gospels: Their Origin and Their Growth.* New York: Harper & Bros., 1957.

HEARD, RICHARD G. *An Introduction to the New Testament.* New York: Harper & Bros., 1950.

HUNTER, ARCHIBALD M. *Introducing the New Testament.* 2nd ed. Philadelphia: The Westminster Press, 1958.

KEE, HOWARD CLARK, and YOUNG, FRANKLIN W. *Understanding the New Testament.* Englewood Cliffs, N. J.: Prentice-Hall, Inc., 1957.

LAYMON, CHARLES. *Great Prayers of the Bible.*[1] Cincinnati, O.: Woman's Division of Christian Service, 1947.

MCNEILE, A. H. *An Introduction to the Study of the New Testament.* 2nd. rev. ed. New York: Oxford University Press, 1953.

METZGER, BRUCE M. *An Introduction to the Apocrypha.* New York: Oxford University Press, 1957.

RICHARDSON, ALAN. *The Miracle-stories of the Gospels.* New York: Harper & Bros., 1942. (Out of print.)

ROWLINGSON, DONALD T. *Introduction to New Testament Study.* New York: The Macmillan Co., 1956.

SCOTT, ERNEST F. *The Purpose of the Gospels.* New York: Charles Scribner's Sons, 1949. (Out of print.)

WRIGHT, G. ERNEST and FILSON, FLOYD V. *Westminster Historical Atlas to the Bible.* Philadelphia: The Westminster Press, 1945.

Studies of Jesus

BARNETT, ALBERT E. *Understanding the Parables of Our Lord.* Naperville, Ill.: Alec R. Allenson, 1954.

BECK, DWIGHT M. *Through the Gospels to Jesus.* New York: Harper & Bros., 1954.

BRANSCOMB, B. HARVIE. *The Teachings of Jesus.* Nashville: Abingdon Press, 1931.

CADBURY, HENRY J. *Jesus: What Manner of Man?* New York: The Macmillan Co., 1947. (Out of print.)

FOSDICK, HARRY EMERSON. *The Man from Nazareth.* New York: Harper & Bros., 1949.

GOODSPEED, EDGAR J. *A Life of Jesus.* New York: Harper & Bros., 1950.

HEARD, GERALD. *A Dialogue in the Desert.* New York: Harper & Bros., c. 1942. (Out of print.)

JOHNSON, SHERMAN E. *Jesus in His Homeland.* New York: Charles Scribner's Sons, 1957.

160

KEPLER, THOMAS S. (ed.) *Contemporary Thinking About Jesus*. Nashville: Abingdon Press, 1944.

KNOX, JOHN. "The Man Christ Jesus," in *Jesus: Lord and Christ*. New York: Harper & Bros., 1958.

LAYMON, CHARLES M. *The Life and Teachings of Jesus*. Nashville: Abingdon Press, 1955.

LAYMON, CHARLES M. *Christ in the New Testament*. Nashville: Abingdon Press, 1958.

MANSON, WILLIAM. *Jesus the Messiah*. Philadelphia: The Westminster Press, 1946. (Out of print.)

ROLLINS, WALLACE E. and ROLLINS, MARION J. *Jesus and His Ministry*. Greenwich, Conn.: The Seabury Press, Inc., 1954.

SCOTT, ERNEST F. *The Lord's Prayer*. New York: Charles Scribner's Sons, 1951.

TAYLOR, VINCENT. *The Life and Ministry of Jesus*. Nashville: Abingdon Press, 1955.

The Gospel of Luke

APPLEGARTH, MARGARET T. *Twelve Baskets Full*.[1] New York: Harper & Bros., 1956.

BALMFORTH, M. A. *The Claredon Bible*. "The Gospel According to Saint Luke." Rev. ed. London: Oxford University Press, 1930.

BARCLAY, WILLIAM. *The Gospel of Luke*. Philadelphia: The Westminster Press, 1956.

CREED, JOHN M. *The Gospel According to St. Luke*. London: Macmillan & Co., Ltd., 1930. (Out of print.)

EASTON, BURTON S. *The Gospel According to St. Luke*. New York: Charles Scribner's Sons, 1926. (Out of print.)

FARRAR, F. W. "The Gospel According to St. Luke," *Cambridge Bible for Schools and Colleges*. New York: Cambridge University Press, 1916. (Out of print.)

GILMOUR, S. M. "The Gospel According to St. Luke," *The Interpreter's Bible*, VIII, 3-434. Nashville: Abingdon Press, 1952.

---

[1] Order from Literature Headquarters, 7820 Reading Road, Cincinnati 37, Ohio.

MAJOR, HENRY and others. *The Mission and Message of Jesus.* New York: E. P. Dutton & Co., Inc., 1948.

MANSON, WILLIAM. *The Gospel of Luke.* The Moffatt New Testament Commentary Series. New York: Harper & Bros., 1930.

PHILLIPS, J. B. "St. Luke's Life of Christ," *The Gospels.* New York: The Macmillan Co., 1953.

NOTES

NOTES